From Suir to Jarama

Mossie Quinlan's Life and Legacy

ORLA
KELLY
PUBLISHING

Liam Cahill

978-1-914225-44-4

Maurice 'Mossie' Quinlan

Rifle No. 715

No. 1 Company

British Battalion

15th International Brigade

Killed In Action, Jarama

17 February 1937

For Eoin and Susan

'You have to believe in something – in a cause that will make the world a better place, or you have wasted your life.'

- Peter O'Connor
Socialist and Anti-Fascist Fighter

Author

Liam Cahill lectures and writes extensively on Irish labour history and contemporary issues. He is a lifelong trade unionist and has held many representative positions in the Labour movement from branch to national level. A former Industrial Reporter, Economics Correspondent and Political Correspondent with RTÉ, Ireland's public broadcaster, he has worked as a public servant and as adviser in government, politics, the private sector and with campaign groups.

He founded and, for many years, edited a popular web site '*An Fear Rua – The GAA Unplugged!*' and is currently an active and influential presence for progressive values on social media. In 2017, he completed the Certificate in Creative and Non-Creative Writing for Publication from Maynooth University.

Author of '*Forgotten Revolution, The Limerick Soviet 1919*' (O'Brien Press, 1990) and '*Forgotten Revolution, The Limerick Soviet 1919 [Centenary Edition]*' (Orla Kelly Publishing, 2019).

Twitter: @LiamCahill2013 @FromSuir2Jarama

CONTENTS

Introduction

At an early stage in researching and writing this book – when I seemed to be floundering in archives, maps and books to little effect – a flash of inspiration came to me: *'Keep your eye on Mossie!'*

So, that is exactly what I have done. I focus on a close and personal description of one man's eighty-three days during the Spanish Civil War, serving with the British Battalion of the 15th International Brigade. Who was he? Why did he volunteer and what were the aftereffects on his grief-stricken family? I touch on the socio-economic and political backgrounds, the high politics and the high military dimension of the war only insofar as I need them to give context to Mossie's experiences. These aspects are already well covered in many other books that I cite in the Source Materials section at the end of this book.

I am inspired and guided in researching and writing this book by the concept of Ethical Remembrance, eloquently advocated and explained by *Uachtarán na hÉireann*, Michael D Higgins. Ethical remembering, the President states, requires us to shine a light on overlooked figures and events, as all of us with intersecting stories attempt to achieve a deeper, more balanced and more inclusive perspective. *'A central dimension of this is a refusal of conscious or unconscious amnesia, not only of persons but also of events and of the assumptions and actions that drove them.'*

President Higgins says that we are all challenged to engage with our shared past in a manner that is honest, authentic and inclusive. *'I believe that we, and those who are part of the discourse with us, must remember in full, taking all of the diverse perspectives and experiences into account, with a willingness to hear the stories that might prove less comfortable, and give space to the perspectives that might challenge each other.'*

My wife, Patricia, died in October 2015, and since then my children and I have weathered many daunting challenges. I dedicate this labour of love to Susie and Eoin in gratitude and pride.

Liam Cahill

30 June 2021

Acknowledgments

I have incurred many debts of profound gratitude in my research and writing. None greater than the one I owe to Seán Kelly, my old friend and comrade from Waterford. I benefitted from Seán's great generosity in sharing his remarkable treasure trove of books, articles, photographs and other materials about the Spanish Civil War. More importantly, he constantly stimulated my thinking and challenged me throughout this project and his insights were invaluable.

Ger McCloskey and David Convery provided the superb photos of present day Jarama that will help readers to orientate themselves within the topography of the battlefield. Rob Cross generously used his skill and experience on the restoration of a 1917 photo of Mossie's grandfather, Alderman Maurice Quinlan, with Éamon de Valera. Thanks go to Dermot Power, whose knowledge and love of Waterford and its history knows no bounds, for his confirmation of the location shown in the only known photograph of Mossie. I am also indebted to my cousins, Mossy Quinlan and his sister Bernie Lara Quinlan, for diligently searching through old family photographs seeking other photos of Mossie.

Dr. Pat McCarthy, the premier historian of revolutionary times in Waterford, kindly provided me with essential information and a reference in official documents about the Quinlan family's continued adherence to the Irish Volunteers and membership of *Sinn Féin* following the John Redmond-induced split in the Volunteers in 1914. Derek Chestnutt provided helpful information and advice on the Quinlan family genealogy and profound thanks are due to John Mernin for sharing his outstanding working in tracing the Quinlan family 'tree' back as far as 1815.

Tony Hennessy drew my attention to an important news report about Mossie's death in the *'Waterford Standard'* newspaper and John Power, a Ballybricken man through and through, talked to me about his memories and insights of Mossie and his family.

I am particularly grateful to Bobby and Breda Brown, in Australia, for identifying and providing information on Bobby Clancy, one of the young men in the photograph with Mossie. Many thanks, as well, to Darren Skelton and the *'Waterford News and Star'* for publicising my efforts to identify the other young men in the photograph. Thanks to Dr. Barry McLoughlin, a recognised authority on Irish involvement in the Spanish Civil War, for his courteous and helpful response to specific queries in relation to Mossie and to Alan Warren in Spain for information in response to a specific factual query.

This book has its roots in a non-fiction essay I submitted as part of my studies at Maynooth University in 2017 for the National University of Ireland Certificate in Creative and Non-Creative Writing for Publication. After many years shackled to 'deadline' journalism and communications, the course liberated me in my approach to writing. From my tutor in Creative Non-Fiction, John MacKenna, I learned that great writing comes from being brave enough to go deep inside yourself and bringing your thoughts and ideas into the open before the 'scrutiny – and judgment – of others. The deeper the journey inside, the greater the vulnerability - but the better the writing.

For reading the book in manuscript and making many insightful and constructive suggestions, my thanks go to John MacKenna, Jim O'Leary, Manus O'Riordan and Seán Kelly.

Since Maynooth, a small group of us have kept in touch and I thank Anthony, Christina, Hazel, Oona and Rosemary for their constancy, inspiration and encouragement. I also acknowledge the support I received from my membership of the Boyne Writers' Group.

Above all, I am profoundly grateful to Mossie's nephew, Mike Quinlan, who contacted me from Britain when he heard that I was researching this book and who generously shared with me his insights and the memories his father, Éamon, had of his childhood and of the eldest brother he admired.

LC

Prologue

It is almost seven months since General Francisco Franco has led Spain's Army of Africa and other elements of the armed forces in revolt against a democratically elected government. Backed by wealthy capitalists, the nobility and feudal landowners, as well as the Catholic Church, Franco seeks to depose the Left-leaning government, end their sweeping reforms and restore the power and privileges of his backers under a Fascist dictatorship led by himself.

Aided by massive quantities of war material and thousands of men despatched by the German Nazi dictator, Adolf Hitler, and the Italian Fascist leader, Benito Mussolini, Franco's Fascist forces sweep up through Southern and Western Spain. His first attempt to take the capital, Madrid, is repulsed by a combination of the Republic's People's Army, volunteers of the International Brigades and local militias.

Franco fixes on another strategy. He already holds all but one of the main roads into and out of Madrid but now he will seek to sever the last remaining open road, the highway from Madrid to Valencia, to where the Republican government has temporarily relocated its capital. The place he chooses to attempt this is at a point on the River Jarama, just South of Madrid. The time is the first week of February 1937.

If his strategy succeeds, he will have a stranglehold on Madrid and he will end the war more quickly.

Chapter One

Jarama

Friday, 12 February 1937

This is the day the olive groves on the slopes of the Jarama valley in Spain become 'an open-air abattoir', in that memorable phrase of the British International Brigader, Jack Jones.

At half past five in the morning, soldiers of the British Battalion, 15th International Brigade, are transferred from the town of Chinchon to a junction where the road from Chinchon to Madrid intersects another road, the one from Morata de Tajuna to San Martin de la Vega. On their way to the front, the men get off the trucks at Villarubia de Santiago and fire off a few rounds into the hills. For most of them, this is the first time they have ever fired a rifle.

A World War One veteran, Captain Tom Wintringham, is the Battalion Commanding Officer. Twenty-five years old Maurice 'Mossie' Quinlan (Rifle No. 715), from South Parade, in Waterford, is in No. 1 Company, commanded by Lieutenant Christopher 'Kit' Conway, a South Tipperary man with a distinguished record in the Irish War of Independence and Irish Civil War. Conway is a former soldier in the British and Irish armies as well as the US National Guard, and a former Training Officer with the IRA. He is a veteran of the battles at Lopera and Las Rozas, near Madrid. No. 1 Company includes a significant number of Irish veterans of the earlier battles who also have experience in the wars at home in Ireland. Harold Fry commands No. 2 (Machine Gun) Company, No. 3 Company is commanded by Bill Briskey and Bert Overton commands No. 4 Company.

At seven o'clock, the men eat breakfast and by ten o'clock they are in their positions for moving forward. They move Westwards in single file in the direction of the Jarama River which lies beyond the next ridge. They trudge up a steep plateau overlooking the river and establish a cookhouse in a nearby farmhouse. As their boots crush the abundant herbs that grow underfoot amid the gorse bushes, the aroma of wild thyme and sage rises around them.

On the march, Fry discovers that his Company has the wrong calibre ammunition for their Maxim machine guns. This will prove a costly mistake in the early part of the battle but, when it is rectified later on, the Maxims will turn the tide back decisively in favour of the Brigaders.

No reconnaissance or scouting of the hills and valley has been carried out and they have no maps. Neither the advancing men, Wintringham, nor Brigade Headquarters are aware that Fascist forces (highly experienced Moroccan troops and Foreign Legionaries of Franco's Army of Africa) are pouring over the river in great numbers since they captured a bridge in the darkness of early morning. They are preparing for an advance on the ridges above it. The Brigaders move forward over a ridge to a narrow sunken road - a five metres wide rut, waist deep, carved out by cartwheels over the centuries in the dusty white soil of the groves. They begin to descend into the river valley in front of them and, for the first time, they come under heavy fire from the Fascist forces.

Out of the West, a flight of Fascist bombers passes overhead on their way to bomb the Republican supply dumps at Morata de Tajuna. Seven Russian fighters respond and scatter the bombers back to their base. Then, the fighters dive to attack the Fascist positions and a dogfight ensues overhead with the Brigaders cheering for the Republican airmen.

A barrage of Fascist machine gun and artillery fire begins and continues for three hours. Nos. 3 and 4 Companies sustain heavy casualties. Shortly before Midday, Mossie and his comrades in No. 1 Company pass through some Spanish infantry being held in reserve. They give the Brigaders chocolate and wine and shout *'Viva las Brigadas Internationales'* as Kit Conway moves his men forward.

It dawns on Wintringham that the Fascists are already across the river and that the offensive he has planned is being turned into a holding action against an unknown force. In fact, he faces three battalions of Moroccans, including a heavy machine gun and mortar company, together with the 6th and 8th *banderas* of the Foreign Legion. The Legion's motto is *'Viva La Muerte!'*, 'Long Live Death!' In all, the Fascists have assembled almost two thousand troops in the sector. Their experience shows in the clever way they make their way upwards from the river. They advance for a distance of two thousand metres, without cover, by exploiting the slightest folds in the ground, bobbing up and down, running and disappearing again. All the while, they maintain continuous and accurate firing.

The British Battalion is outnumbered by more than three to one and is heavily outgunned as well. Wintringham wants to halt their advance on the ridge overlooking the river but George Nathan, the Brigade's Assistant Chief of Staff, and runners arriving from Brigade HQ overrule this and order the volunteers to continue on through the descending open ground.

In the long grass of the valley, there are two hills ahead – each of them not more than ten metres high. The one to the left is flat topped, thickly wooded with low thorn trees and capped by a small, white-washed farmhouse. The men of Overton's No. 4 Company advance towards it. The other is a steep conical hill, sparsely covered in grass, low gorse bushes and wild thyme. Less than half a kilometre further to the right, isolated and perfectly symmetrical, is a third rise that comes to be known as the Knoll.

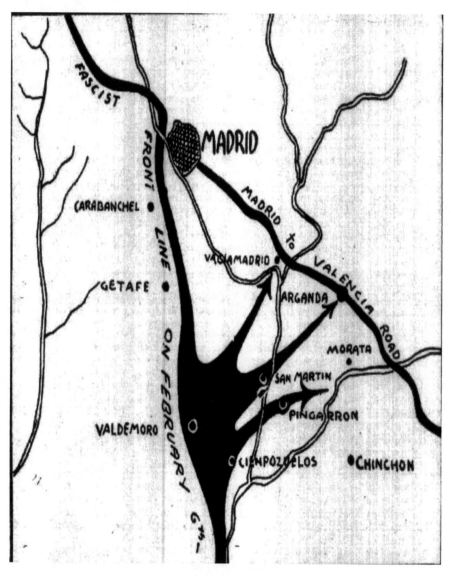

Map of the Fascist front lines on the morning of 6 February 1937 as Franco's forces begin their three-pronged attack across the Jarama River to try to cut the Madrid to Valencia Road and surround the capital. *(RGASPI Archives 545/2/405/20 , Page 38 of Frank Ryan's 'The Book of the XV Brigade')*

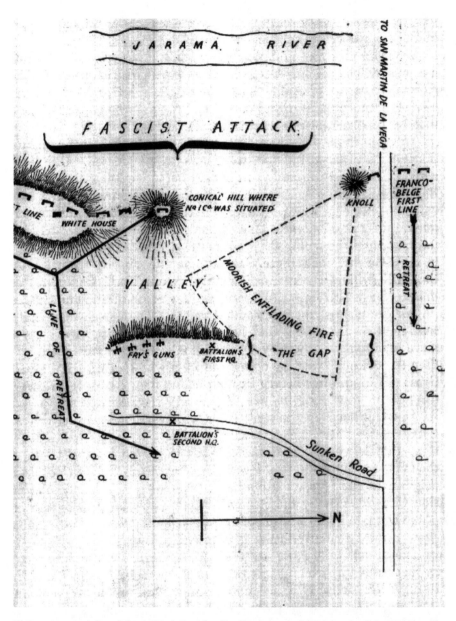

This map is reproduced from Frank Ryan's officially sanctioned 'The Book of the XV Brigade, Records of British, American, Canadian and Irish Volunteers in Spain 1936-38'. *(RGASPI Archives 545/2/405/26 and RGASPI Archives 545/3/465/10)*

No. 1 Company is still in the olive groves. Emerging from them, Conway calls a meeting of his section commanders. He says he intends to take up a position on the Knoll but a Brigade runner tells him to realign his advance closer to Overton on his left. Turning forty-five degrees to the Southeast, Conway heads towards the Conical Hill.

Around 12.30 pm, No. 1 and No. 4 Companies reach the reserve slopes. Conway and Overton order their men to spread out and an eight hundred metres long line is formed. Once on the summits, they pass down the far side onto the rolling scrub land beyond. Several hundred metres away, the lead units of the Fascist troops of Lieutenant Colonel Carlos Asensio Cabanillas, a forty-one-year-old career officer, can be seen pouring over the San Martin bridge in trucks and cars and beginning their advance up the slope from the river.

Silhouetted against the skyline, the British and Irish Brigaders are easy targets for the Nazi German Condor Legion's heavy machine guns that support the Fascist advance. On the Western slopes of the two hills, several men are hit by the raking fire. It hits them before they know what is happening. The rest just walk on but all around, men continue to slump to the ground, hit in the legs, chest, stomach or head.

In No. 1 Company, some of Mossie's comrades are also falling but Kit Conway takes charge of the situation and their battle experience is standing to them. Conway runs from group to group directing their fire, calling out ranges and pointing to targets with his cane. Initially, some of his men take cover but the thick bushes studding the forward slope of the hill obscure their view. 'Don't lie down!', Conway calls out. 'Stand up and show you're not afraid of the Fascist bastards.'

Conway's position on the Conical Hill, though, is becoming untenable. The Moroccans, dodging through the long grass and hollows in the rising ground, are closing in and their fire is becoming increasingly accurate. Exposed on the forward slope, the men of No. 1 Company make easy targets and they are being slaughtered. Conway orders them to retreat to the top of the hill. It offers little cover but its height gives a small advantage.

In places, the thin, white soil on the summit is almost bare and elsewhere there is grass and weeds, but the shoots are only a couple of centimetres high. The men try to shelter from the hail of bullets by pressing themselves into the contours of the hilltop. Ignoring the whizzing bullets, Conway paces the hilltop firing his rifle and shouting commands.

At one o'clock in the afternoon, Harold Fry's machine gun company reach their designated position on the ridge and, to their right, it drops so steeply that there is an area of dead ground. They take up position behind a low stone wall. They have an excellent field of fire and can command the entire valley. Fry's orders are to concentrate fire on the Knoll and prevent any further advances by the Moroccans.

At around the same time, to support further advance by the Moroccans, Lieutenant Colonel Asensio Cabanillas orders an artillery barrage across the Brigaders' positions. The white house on the little hill is an easy target. After two shots to find the correct range, the third shell scores a direct hit and the gunners begin to pepper the hill with shells. Men are slaughtered. Dead bodies lie everywhere and body parts rain down onto the rear slopes. The shattered walls of the white house are smeared with blood and gore. The commander of No. 4 Company, Overton, panics and flees.

To the right of No. 1 Company on the Conical Hill, the Moroccans outflank Conway's men. They take the unoccupied Knoll and catch the Brigaders in crossfire. Now, No. 1 Company comes under heavy artillery and mortar fire. The summit of the hill is literally being blown away. At 2.30 pm the inevitable happens. Conway is hit. Three machine gun bullets rip open his groin and, as his weapon spins from his hands, he crumples to the ground. A Dubliner, Jim Prendergast, a veteran of Lopera and Las Rozas, rushes forward to him. Conway's face is drained of colour, his flesh taut with agony. Before the medics carry him away, he urges his men to do their best and hold on. Then, as Prendergast wipes away a tear, Conway is stretchered away to the rear.

Not long afterwards, Prendergast himself is wounded and ends up in the same ambulance as Kit Conway. He speaks briefly with him and, the following morning, he is told that Conway is dead. Thus ends the chequered life of this charismatic and colourful leader. His first fourteen years of life are as an orphan in a poorhouse, he then works for a farmer for a pittance, his upkeep and an occasional suit of clothes. His Commandant in the 6th Battalion, 3rd Tipperary Brigade of the IRA, Tommy Ryan, describes him as 'fearless and a natural born fighter', 'the white-haired boy of Seán Hogan's Flying Column.' By the time he arrives in Spain to lead his men with such distinction and great gallantry, he is an active member of the Building Workers' Section of the Irish Transport and General Workers' Union[1] and a seasoned veteran of strikes and disputes with the employers. He is counted among the great heroes of Jarama.

Ken Stalker takes command of the Company and moves them back to the South side of the Conical Hill and then further on to the White House Hill (later, dubbed 'Suicide Hill'). As they begin to ascend it, the late winter sun begins to set. A battalion of Moroccan troops starts to advance on them and they start to withdraw from the hill.

In the late afternoon, at least fifty machine guns are trained and firing on the Internationals' positions. Down on the valley floor, the remnants of No.1 and No. 4 Companies are retreating. Dozens of them are gunned down. Ken Stalker is shot through the head and

---

[1] Merged in 1990 with the Federated Workers' Union of Ireland to form SIP-TU, Ireland's largest trade union.

killed. An Anglicised Egyptian born volunteer, André Diamant, takes over command of No. 1 Company. Already tempered in the fighting at Lopera, Diamant is one of the few men who does not panic. He asks for volunteers to fight a rear-guard action to cover the retreat. Thirty men step forward and they remain in the valley for half an hour as their comrades draw back. The last stragglers of the No. 1 and No. 4 Companies retreat through the olive groves to the South of the British line. They are joined by remnants of Briskey's No. 3 Company, whose commanding officer has been shot dead.

By six o'clock in the evening, the sun is setting beyond the hills on the far, Western banks of the Jarama and darkness is falling rapidly. Five hundred Moroccans and Foreign Legionaries advance from the White House Hill but Harold Fry's Maxims are now loaded with the correct ammunition and are readied and awaiting them. The 'spare' officer of No. 1 Company, Fred Copeman (a Royal Navy veteran) has cowed Fry into silence because of the earlier mix-up over the ammunition. Copeman has trained these crews in the rudiments of machine gunning at the British HQ in Madrigueras and he takes command.

The Fascists are spread out as they advance in a long line. They are led by mounted officers with flowing red and blue cloaks and sabres drawn. When the enemy are only fifty metres from the Battalion line, Copeman gives the order to open fire. Within sixty seconds, five Maxims sweep from right to left pounding more than a thousand bullets into the Fascists in three minutes.

They fall like mown wheat. As they turn and run, Copeman orders the gunners to fire into their path of retreat to prevent them escaping. When they fall to the ground and play dead, his gunners continue to fire at them. As the firing stops, more than half the Fascists lie dead and dying on the valley floor. The cries of wounded men mingle with the whinnying of distressed horses.

Darkness deepens on the first evening of the battle and a thin sliver of a sickle moon rises over Jarama. A British volunteer, David Crook, always remembers it: 'Throughout the last fifty years, I've never seen such a moon without thinking of Jarama.'

At the beginning of the day, the British Battalion had deployed four hundred riflemen into battle. Now, under the darkness, a hundred of them lie dead and a hundred and forty-five are wounded. Around 7 pm, André Diamant leads a large group of survivors of No. 1, No. 3 and No. 4 Companies, defiantly singing the *Internationale*, back to the Battalion HQ at the Sunken Road. Diamant has emerged as a natural leader after, first, Conway, and then, Stalker are shot. In all, Wintringham is left with two hundred and twenty-five men.

Mossie Quinlan, from Waterford, has survived his first day in Jarama's charnel house.

Like all the riflemen, he is exhausted and the night is bitterly cold. At eight o'clock, the Battalion Quartermaster, Josh Francis, arrives in his red Studebaker truck loaded with food, picks and shovels. There is soup, hot coffee and cold boiled rice. After their meal, Mossie and his comrades settle down to catch a few hours of sleep before their next day in battle begins.

Saturday, 13th February 1937

At two o'clock in the morning, André Diamant and Fred Copeman return to the Sunken Road with about thirty stragglers rounded up from the Cookhouse. At 3 am, the Battalion stands to. A truck arrives with more food and supplies.

There is plenty of hot sweet coffee and thick bully beef sandwiches. George Aitken, the Battalion Commissar, is with the truck.

As they face into the second day of the battle, there are two hundred and twenty-five men remaining in the British Battalion. Mossie

Quinlan is one of fifty-eight men of No. 1 Company under the command of André Diamant. No. 1 Company is deployed to the far left of the British positions, towards the South of the sector. Bert Overton and the fifty-five survivors of No. 4 Company take up positions a hundred metres to the right of Harold Fry's No. 2 Company of Maxim machine guns on the ridge.

From there, No. 4 Company can cover the dead ground that snakes up from the valley floor to the rear of the machine guns. The remnants of No. 3 Company are sent down the Sunken Road to the right. Tom Wintringham and his staff take up their position two hundred metres behind Fry's gunners, not far from the Sunken Road. On a bitterly cold morning, Moroccan troops attack at dawn but are again beaten off by the Maxim machine gunners. After the failure of this initial advance, a quiet lull begins.

Fascist bombers fly overhead at half past ten to bomb the nearby Republican-held town of Morata de Tajuna. Republican fighters down two of them and the others flee. Then, some Russian bombers pass over, high up, and their fighter escorts strafe the Fascist lines. At around one o'clock in the afternoon, three Republican bombers attack Suicide Hill where the White House is situated. To the North of the British sector, the Dimitrov, Thaelmann and Franco-Belge Battalions are under strong pressure from renewed Fascist attacks.

Wintringham recalls advice he was given during his service with the British Army in the Great War. He leads thirty men in a feint attack to the left and leaves the Commissar, George Aitken, in command. The objective is to open fire on the White House on Suicide Hill and make the Fascists believe that a counterattack is imminent.

If this works, it will ease the pressure on the other battalions to the North. Meanwhile, Russian T26 tanks chase enemy troops from the plateau.

At three o'clock, Wintringham receives a phone message from the Brigade Commander, Colonel János Gálicz: 'Advance at once, regardless of tank support'. He ignores the order knowing that he does not have the men required for this task, nor the promised tank, artillery or air support required for an effective advance. Aitken's feint to the left, to draw Fascist fire from the White House and ease the pressure to the North, is petering out. Northwards, to the right of the British sector, the Dimitrovs are falling back further and the gap between them and the British section of the line is widening.

At four o'clock, Wintringham returns to Aitken's position and orders him to withdraw an hour later to the Sunken Road. At the appointed time, Aitken's contingent begins to withdraw in pairs, at five-minute intervals, so as not to alert the Moroccans to what is happening. Wintringham gives a similar order to Diamant and his No. 1 Company on the left flank but they are not to begin to begin their withdrawal until 5.30pm. For Mossie Quinlan and his comrades it has been a relatively quiet day but – because of their isolated position on the flank - they have received no food.

As he makes these dispositions, Wintringham is unaware that accurate artillery fire has been raining down on Overton's No. 4 Company who are positioned between Harold Fry's No. 2 (Machine Gun) Company and Fascist troops advancing in the dead land to the right of their position. Overton, whose actions at Jarama veer between cowardice and confusion, flees towards the rear. He is immediately followed by his fifty men. This leaves Fry and his machine gunners totally exposed to a Fascist attack from their right, along the top of the ridge.

At 4.30 pm Wintringham receives a message from Fry saying that he has observed the Fascist commander in position on the front, seemingly preparing to attack. Unaware of the defection of No. 4 Company, the Captain is satisfied that he has his men in place to hold the line and repel the expected attack. Suddenly, the artillery falls silent and the Fascists launch their attack.

With no Brigaders to block their path, Moroccan troops of the Fascist army draw near to the tired and confused gunners of No. 2 Company. They approach the position with clenched fists or singing the *Internationale*. Some of the Brigaders are fooled and welcome the Fascists, believing that they are reinforcements. Moroccans and Foreign Legionaries pour into the machine gun emplacements. Within minutes, the fighting is over and twenty-seven Brigaders are taken prisoner and their machine guns captured.

From the top of the ridge, the Fascist troops turn the Maxim guns on the British volunteers who are below them in the Sunken Road. Hundreds of Fascist riflemen use snub nosed dum-dum bullets to inflict terrible wounds. Tom Wintringham is wounded in the leg. Overton, temporarily regaining courage again, leads a foolhardy charge of forty men up the hill against the Fascist positions. Only six of them come back, including Overton himself. Foreign Legionaries remain to operate the captured Maxims while the Moroccans escort the prisoners away. Fortunately for their survival, they are handed over to the *Guardia Civil* police rather than left to the cruel attentions of the Moroccans.

In the Sunken Road there is panic. The Commissar, George Aitken, takes over command of the Battalion. Twelve men volunteer to secure the right flank. The crew of the sole Maxim remaining in British hands joins the men in the Sunken Road. They await the next onslaught.

With darkness falling, the firing dies down on the Sunken Road. There are wounded men lying everywhere and morale is low. Aitken sends No. 1 Company to patrol the left flank of the British position where they manage to link up with elements of the Republican Lister Brigade who are holding the line to the South. Not long after nightfall, a single Fascist flare drops on the battalion's ammunition store and causes a huge explosion. There is smoke and noise everywhere. Overton leads another panicked retreat from the Sunken Road and almost half the battalion are missing.

Jock Cunningham, the original commander of No. 1 Company, arrives at the Cookhouse between dusk and midnight. He has been suffering from flu since the Battalion's arrival in Chinchon on 9 February and - still sick with fever - he drags himself from his bed and hitches a lift to the front line in an ambulance. He is a few hundred metres away from the front when he hears the massive explosion. He encounters some of the men fleeing with Overton and, because he is 'idolised by his comrades', manages to calm them and they join a growing band of about fifty or sixty troops that he leads back to the frontline.

Cunningham is shocked by what he finds at the Sunken Road. About a hundred men are asleep except for a few shivering sentries leaning on their rifles. He shakes the men awake and, as the dawn comes up, they are heartened by the presence of their charismatic, experienced leader and their morale is lifted. Cunningham is a former member of the Argyll and Sutherland Highlanders and is a veteran of the battles at Madrid, Lopera and Las Rozas. 'Handsome and loveable and as tough as they come', is Fred Copeman's assessment of him.

Among the sleeping men is Mossie Quinlan, of Waterford. He has come through his second day in the cauldron of Jarama and will shortly face into the next one.

Sunday, 14ᵗʰ February 1937

Jock Cunningham begins the day by leading a charge up the slope to the ridge to where the Fascists are manning the Battalion's captured Maxims. They surprise a company of Moroccans - who flee - and the Internationals recapture some of the machine guns and pull back with them. At this point, the Battalion is just over two hundred men strong. Cunningham withdraws them in two stages from the Sunken Road to the higher ground behind it. As the Maxim crews set up their guns, the riflemen nervously cover them and then withdraw themselves.

At nine o'clock, Colonel Gálicz orders Cunningham to re-occupy the Sunken Road and he complies reluctantly. The Battalion spends the rest of the morning improving their defences. Their numbers are strengthened as Diamant's No. 1 Company returns from their posting on the left flank and by three hundred seasoned Spanish troops from the battle-hardened Lister Battalion on the left. Further reinforcements arrive from Morata de Tajuna, members of the Brigade Guard, who are veterans of the fighting at Lopera and Las Rozas. The machine guns are in place and along the Sunken Road the Battalion holds a line about 1.5 kilometres long. Morale is boosted by the arrival of a delivery of some letters from home.

The courageous and resourceful commander of Mossie Quinlan's No. 1 Company, André Diamant, discusses the Battalion's position with Cunningham and they agree to withdraw the Company to the olive trees on the other side of the road behind the Battalion's positions. After they relocate, Diamant walks up and down the line four times to do a headcount. Two hundred and fifteen men of the British Battalion remain.

By Midday, it is very hot and the men have no water. They begin collecting urine to cool the Maxim guns later on. In the early afternoon, the Fascist artillery opens up and the enemy advances in strength with captured Russian T26 tanks on the Southern, or left, flank of the Sunken Road. They drive up along the Sunken Road, firing as they go.

The Spanish troops fighting with the Internationals break rank and the left flank crumbles. Thousands of Moroccan infantry follow the tanks and they have cover from aeroplanes and the Nazi Condor Legion machine gunners. A terrifying slaughter begins. Dead and wounded men fall everywhere and the Moroccans bayonet the wounded to death, sometimes inflicting up to twenty slashes of the blade. Panic spreads and the British centre and right flank begins to crumble.

Jock Cunningham is one of the last to withdraw. Bob Hilliard from Killarney, County Kerry, once ordained as a Church of Ireland minister, and three other brave Internationals stand their ground. Armed only with rifles, they face the advancing tanks. The three are killed and Hilliard is fatally wounded.

André Diamant and the remnants of No. 1 Company are holding out, fighting a rear-guard action. He has thirty men whom he withdraws in controlled stages. After firing from one position for several minutes, they pull back to the next ridgeline, where once again they take cover and open fire. In this way, he and his men hold up the enemy advance five or six times. At 4.30 pm, Diamant and his men reach their final position – a ridge on the edge of the olive groves. To the East, the Cookhouse is visible and beyond it lies the Madrid to Valencia Road, the Fascists' objective. To buy time for the last of the wounded to be carried down the hill to the rear, Diamant forms a defensive line with heavy stones.

From behind these, the men snipe at any targets that become visible. Despite being under very heavy fire, No. 1 Company have the crest of the hill more or less under control. After holding their position for a considerable time, Diamant gives the order to withdraw. Picking themselves up, the men make their way down the slope to the Cookhouse. Nothing now stands between the Fascists and the Valencia Road.

All day, the Cookhouse is in turmoil but Alex 'Tiny' Silverman and his cooks keep cooking. Amid rumours of a general retreat along the front line, men are slipping away. Groups of mixed nationalities are falling back along the road to Morata de Tajuna with little or no organisation. Aitken returns from consulting with senior officers at Morata. On his way back, he encounters more than twenty British volunteers and, at gunpoint, forces them back towards the line. By the time he arrives back at the Cookhouse, the situation is deteriorating further. It is a scene of extreme confusion. The buildings and olive groves are filled with dead, wounded and dying men. Bemused survivors, mostly from the British Battalion, are milling around the courtyard.

Captain Frank Ryan, Commissar of the Irish volunteers in the 15th Brigade, is at the Cookhouse trying to impose some sort of order. A young Spanish officer, his hand slightly wounded, is pleading with his men and then threatening them with his automatic pistol. Ryan firmly takes charge. Through his interpreter, he orders the Spaniards to form up. They stumble to their feet and others join them. Cunningham is also organising troops and Ryan marches his group towards them. Cunningham orders a headcount and finds that they muster a hundred and forty men. Having come through Hell in the previous two days, these men are determined to resist the Fascist advance.

Ryan and Cunningham leave the wounded at the Cookhouse and lead their men Northwards towards the junction with the San Martin – Morata Road. There, they turn West along this road as the sun sinks into the olive groves ahead of them. To raise morale and stiffen resolve, Ryan urges the men to 'Sing Up!' and leads them in the *Internationale*. There is a remarkable transformation. Quaveringly at first, then more lustily, then in one resounding chant, the international workers' anthem rises from the ranks, Mossie Quinlan's voice among them. Bent backs are straightened and tired legs begin to march sturdily.

What was a routed rabble a short time ago now marches into battle again as proudly as they had done a few days earlier.

As the column advances, its numbers swell. Spaniards and other nationalities come out to see and cheer them and they too begin to sing. Men streaming back from the front line stop and join them. There are French and Slav volunteers from other battalions and soon the

Internationale is being sung in several languages. Others are shouting *'No Pasaran!'*

As they march along the road towards the front line, they encounter a solitary figure – the Commander of the 15ᵗʰ International Brigade, Colonel Gálicz. He makes a quiet, sensible speech. Gálicz tells them that the decisive moment has come. He needs them to fill a gap in the line because he has no other unit available. Cunningham smartly salutes the Colonel and replies 'We'll go up and fill that gap'. He tells the men they could be facing certain death if they return to the line but the Colonel has asked for their help. No one refuses to follow him and they are joined by another Spanish unit to their right.

Cunningham knows they must swing left to fill the gap but he is not familiar with the road. Finally, at dusk, they emerge several hundred metres behind the Fascist line. In darkness, the next few hours are chaotic and confusing. The men advance individually or in small groups. With bullets whizzing overhead, they crawl on their stomachs for three hundred metres, shoulder to shoulder, packed tightly. Hearing troops advancing behind them, the Moroccans begin to panic. Their most advanced guards run without firing a shot. Only some hours earlier, they thought the British are broken. Now, they are being attacked by an unknown number. Maybe this is the general Republican counterattack they have been dreading?

Orders are being shouted to the Internationals in several languages. Ryan checks the correct words with his interpreter and begins to give orders in Spanish - *'Adalente!* Forward! and *'Abajo!* Down!' Calmly, a portly French officer leads his men forward towards the flickering barrels of the German machine guns. They crawl to within striking distance and then fall on the gunners with fixed bayonets.

Men are stumbling and tripping over dead bodies in the dark. After tripping over a corpse at his feet, Frank Ryan identifies it as one of their own volunteers. He realises that they have regained their old lines. He gives the order to halt and dig in. Working through the night, the troops construct a series of rifle pits strung out in a rough line through the olive groves.

Dawn breaks. It is clear that the counterattack led by Ryan and Cunningham is successful. On the left, they make contact with the Lister Battalion and to their right, the Dimitrovs have also forced the Fascists back. All along the line, the enemy is held. For now, at least, the Madrid to Valencia Road is secure.

In No. 1 Company, Mossie Quinlan has come through his third day in battle.

Tuesday, 16 February 1937, Wednesday 17 February 1937

On opposite sides of a dusty country road in Spain, not too far south of Madrid, two young Irishmen encounter each other for a few moments. Maurice 'Mossie' Quinlan is a survivor of three of the most harrowing days of slaughter in the Spanish Civil War. At Jarama, the International Brigades and their Spanish comrades have defeated Franco's grand strategy to end the war early by surrounding and cutting off Madrid from the rest of the democratic Spanish Republic, but at a high price in lost lives and wounded.

Peter O'Connor is a volunteer in the American Lincoln Battalion. Although he opposes it, Peter accepts a controversial majority decision at a meeting of some Irish volunteers in January to leave the British Battalion and fight with the Americans instead. Having arrived at Jarama on Monday, 15 February, from their training base at Villanueva de la Jara, the Americans are moving into positions the following day to reinforce the front line and preserve the Madrid to Valencia Road.

Mossie and Peter are pals since they were kids at home in Waterford in *Fianna Éireann*, the boy scouts wing of the Irish Republican Army.

Both are veterans of the IRA itself, the Waterford Workers' Study Group, then the breakaway, socialist Irish Republican Congress, and later, the Communist Party of Ireland and the Communist Party of Great Britain.

Peter is resting with some comrades on the side of a hill as a column of British Battalion volunteers moves along the road below in single file to another section of the line. He spots Mossie among the group. Mossie is wearing a French-made Adrian helmet and a trench coat because there is still more than a touch of Winter chill in the air on the plateau of central Spain.

The landscape through which he marches is bleached to a shade of light ochre by centuries of searing sunshine and sparse rainfall. Olive trees respond well to long dry summers. They thrive in soil that has good drainage. On the hills near Madrid, they are planted from the bottom to the top. They begin sparsely enough but soon the slopes are thickly covered with dense groves of dark green olive trees all the way to the top. Paradoxically, from this inhospitable environment comes an abundant crop of life-enhancing olives.

Peter calls out a comradely greeting and receives a shouted response. The line is moving so there is no time for the two men to exchange even a few words. This is the last Peter sees of him, despite several attempts to establish contact.

On a Thursday, possibly 18 February, but less likely the 25 February, he meets a Belfast chap from No. 1 Company who tells him that a sniper shot Mossie in the head after only a day in the front lines.

In his *'Book of the XV Brigade'*, Captain Frank Ryan, Commissar of the Irish volunteers, recalls Mossie being shot through the head by a sniper while attempting to rescue a wounded comrade from between the lines. When he is killed, Mossie is exactly a month away from his 26th birthday on Saint Patrick's Day and is just over eighty days in Spain.

News of Mossie's death travels back very slowly to Waterford. Just over five weeks after he is killed, the *'Irish Press'* newspaper of 20 March 1937 reports his death in a page one 'lead' story. The headline reads, *'Two More Irish Casualties in Spain'*. The subheadlines say, *'Ex-IRA Man a Victim'*, *'Killed in Battle for Valencia Road'* and *'Italian Rout Reported'*. The report reads:

'Two more Irishmen have been killed while serving with the International Brigade on the Government side in Spain. They are:

Maurice R Quinlan (34), South Parade, Waterford;

James Foley, Poplar, London.

According to reports received in Dublin yesterday, the two were killed when General Mangada, to whose Division they were attached, flung his reserves against the Insurgent forces now striving to cut the Madrid-Valencia road.

Aged 34, Mr Quinlan was a well-known commercial traveller in Waterford.

Mr. Foley was 36. He was a member of the Dublin Brigade, IRA, during the Anglo-Irish War, but he refused to take sides in the Civil War and went to London where he worked as a docker.'

This is how Mossie's father, his stepmother and the rest of his family first hear of his death.

On the same day, short reports are carried on page 1 of the *'Irish Times'*, in the *'Belfast Telegraph'* and there is a report too in the *'Waterford Standard'* on 27 March. The similarity of wording suggests that they are all based on the same despatch from one of the international news agencies with a representative in Spain.

Although its founder, Éamon De Valera, as head of the government, is pursuing a policy of support for non-intervention in the war, the *'Irish Press'* is more measured in its coverage. It refers factually to 'the Government side in Spain' and describes Franco's troops as 'the Insurgent forces'. The other newspapers reporting Mossie's death are also more nuanced, reflecting their orientation towards their mainly Protestant readership. Not surprisingly, no report is carried in the *'Irish Independent'*, the most vociferous supporter of Franco and most vituperative opponent of the Spanish Republic among the Irish newspapers.

The newspaper reports illustrate the perils of regarding journalism – especially from a war zone - as 'the first draft of history'. Mossie's age is incorrectly given as thirty-four. His middle initial is given as 'R' but his second name is Patrick.

Two days after the reports in the Dublin newspapers, Mossie's uncle, Charles Quinlan – who practises as a solicitor in Waterford – writes to JW Dulanty, the Irish Free State High Commissioner in London. He states that Mossie's father has read newspaper reports 'that his son had been killed while fighting with the International Brigades formed under the *aegis* of the Valencia government. My client has no official confirmation of this fact and I shall be obliged if, on his behalf, you will ascertain from the responsible authority in London if the report was true and what was the date of his death.'

Dulanty immediately sends a message – marked 'Urgent' - to Joseph Walshe, Secretary of the Irish Department of External Affairs, in Dublin, forwarding a copy of Charles's letter. Dulanty says that the Spanish embassy in London 'have no information regarding casualties in the forces serving under the Spanish government and have suggested that enquiry should be made of the International Brigades' headquarters in Valencia. He continues: 'I have thought it better to convey this information to the Department rather than direct to Mr. Quinlan, as it may be that the Department, through Mr Kerney[2], has machinery at hand for the expeditious making of such enquiries.'

---

[2] Leopold H Kerney, Irish Ambassador to Spain, 1 January 1935 to 31 December 1946

On 15 April, Joseph Walshe tells Charles Quinlan that 'Enquiries are being made regarding the fate of Mr. Quinlan and as soon as information is received a further communication will be addressed to you.' On the same date, an Assistant Secretary in the Department – a very senior official - writes to the Chancellor of the Spanish Legation in Dublin informing her that, following the newspaper reports, a query has been received from Mossie's father about his death. Seán Murphy writes: 'I am to request that you may be so good as to have enquiries made regarding the truth of this report and, if true, the date and circumstances of Mr. Quinlan's death.'

Two days later, the Chancellor, Mary Conway, replies that she has forwarded the query to the Ministry of State in Valencia. When no reply is received, Walshe sends a reminder and two days later the Chancellor replies that the Ministry of State has not responded and that a further reminder will be sent.

There is no further correspondence in the Department's file nor is there any indication that the officials involved consult with their Minister, Éamon De Valera, who holds the politically sensitive portfolio of External Affairs along with his position as President of the Executive Council of the Irish Free State. Had they done so, he might notice that the solicitor appealing for information is a prominent member and legal adviser to the opposition Fine Gael party in Waterford. But would he also know that the young man killed in Spain is a grandson of a friend and colleague who stood with him in torrential rain on a *Sinn Féin* platform outside Waterford in 1917?

Jarama's aftermath

Fierce fighting continues in the Jarama sector until 27 February when the Fascists beat off a doomed Republican counterattack, spearheaded by the recently arrived American Abraham Lincoln Battalion. In attacks on 23 as well as 27 February, they suffer horrific losses – a hundred and twenty-seven Brigaders killed and two hundred wounded. However, the positions regained by the British Battalion on the third night of combat are held until the war ends.

Both sides dig in and the battle slows to a defensive stalemate, reminiscent of the Western Front in the Great War. It is probably on one of the very early days of this deadlock, with both sides dug in defensively and snipers active, that one shoots Mossie Quinlan as he crawls into no-man's land to rescue a comrade. The stalemate means that Franco's strategy to finish the war quickly is in tatters.

The dead of Jarama comprise twenty thousand Fascists and twenty-five thousand Republicans. Of the five hundred British and Irish volunteers who advance into battle on 12 February, one hundred and fifty are dead and a similar number are wounded. Spanish replacements fill out a Company in the Battalion to make up the numbers and the majority of the Battalion remains in position until June.

Jock Cunningham is wounded on 14 March, promoted to Major and assigned a Staff role in Brigade command. On 23 March, George Aitken is promoted to Brigade Commissar of the 15th International Brigade. On 27 April, Bert Overton, the former Commanding Officer of No.4 Company is court martialled and sentenced to work in a labour battalion, a fate that later leads to his death in the Battle of Brunete, while carrying ammunition to a forward position.

On the afternoon of 29 April, the sector is quiet and only a few Battalion comrades are in the trenches keeping watch. There is the occasional whine and crash of a shell or rifle grenade and explosive bullets regularly burst the air. The rest of the Battalion is lined up in military formation a few metres behind the trenches. It is a memorial service for fallen comrades whose roughly made graves are all around. The graves have been respectfully tended with flowers planted and each bears the name of a buried comrade.

In the centre, there is a cairn of stones in the shape of the Republic's five-pointed star. There are flowers on this, as well, and a roughly shaped board displays the names of the fallen who lie nearby. The inscription reads '*In memory of Comrades who fell in this sector. They laid down their lives for democracy*'. At each point of the star a soldier stands resting on his downward turned rifle, with bowed head. Two of the five are members of the Battalion's recently assigned Spanish company. Nearby, another Brigader holds aloft the flag of the embattled Republic.

At three o'clock, the new Battalion Commanding Officer, Fred Copeman, and the Battalion Commissar, George Aitken, reverently lay wreaths on the cairn, stand with bowed heads and then turn away. Aitken speaks:

> '*They were our friends. We had come to know them intimately. They shared our joys and our sorrows in the days of training. They fought side by side with us in fierce battles.*
>
> *They lived with us day and night in the trenches, shared the same dugouts, stood on guard by our side, shivered with us in the cold nights and huddled close to us when, on many a night the rain poured down in torrents. How could we help growing fond of them and sorrowing at their passing? They lie here now, sleeping their long last sleep*'.

CHAPTER TWO

<u>Mossie Goes to Spain</u>

Sometime in the earlier part of December 1936, Mossie Quinlan goes to the Head Office of the Communist Party of Great Britain behind the Covent Garden fruit market, in London, to volunteer to fight in Spain with the International Brigades. He is closely questioned about his reasons and motivation for volunteering, probably by either 'Robbie' Robson, a veteran of the Great War, or Johnny Campbell, an experienced party worker with a formidable reputation. Mossie is exactly the type of volunteer they are looking for – sound Communist politics, in his mid-twenties, unmarried and, from his time in the IRA in Ireland, some familiarity with military training and discipline.

He is given a date to report to Victoria Station on a particular evening where he is met by a representative of the CPGB and is given rail and boat tickets for France plus a small number of Francs to buy food along the way. He is part of a small group of volunteers who pretend to be on a day trip to Dunkirk, for which no passport is necessary. At midnight, the group catches the mail boat from Dover. They endure a rough crossing of the wintry English Channel, trying in vain to catch some sleep on the rough wooden benches.

Tired and tense from their sea crossing, from Dunkirk they take a train to Arras where they change trains for Amiens. They make another change at Amiens, this time for the train that takes them all the way to the *Gare Du Nord* in Paris, arriving in the early afternoon. Mossie and the other volunteers make their way separately by taxi to the *Bureau des Syndicats,* the headquarters of the Communist trade union, the *Confédération Générale du Travail,* in Montmarte. The *Bureau* is the assembly point for International Brigades volunteers from all over Europe. It is filled with feverish activity and a babble of different languages.

The volunteers are medically examined, they are questioned closely about their political affiliations and are given a talk about the dangers they face. When that is over, they are offered the option of turning back. One or two change their mind but the rest remain committed. After overnighting in a cheap hotel, they are given a railway ticket for the town of Perpignan, close to the border with Spain. This involves another complex rail journey – the evening train from the *Gare d'Austerlitz* to the Mediterranean port of Marseille, then another train from there to Perpignan.

In the afternoon of the next day, a weary and ill-assorted group of young men from many European countries steps off the train. Members of the local Communist Party bring them to a hall for a hot meal and then they are put on a bus to cross over the Pyrenees by an unapproved road, guided by a Communist from Perpignan. It is a bitterly cold night and, as the bus climbs through the brooding, snow-capped mountains, a heavy snow or frost glistens in the moonlight. The passengers are tense. They travel part of the way without lights and in strict silence until they cross the border, then they burst into loud cheers and begin signing the *Internationale* and other revolutionary songs. After a few hours, the bus stops at the town of Figueras and Mossie and the other volunteers step on to Spanish soil for the first time. It is an emotional moment for them and for the Spanish comrades who greet them enthusiastically.

As Mossie and his comrades arrive in Spain on 21 December 1936, the rebellion against the elected government is in its fifth month. It begins on 17 July 1936 when the veteran General José Sanjurjo leads the Army of Africa in revolt. Three days later, Sanjurjo is killed in a plane crash, near Lisbon, and General Francisco Franco begins moves to fill the gap in leadership.

The rebellion is intended to topple Spain's Popular Front government, *El Frente Popular*, an electoral coalition of Republicans, the *Partido Communista Espana* and Socialists.

It is in power since a general election on 6 February 1936. The Communist International – the Comintern – Stalin's instrument for promoting Communism worldwide and enhancing Soviet influence, endorses the concept of the popular front. Where Fascism is a threat, Communists must face into it, oppose it and ally themselves with democratic political forces. The Spanish Anarchists give the government conditional support. The Popular Front is committed to extending workers' rights, reforming landholding, curbing the role of the Catholic church in education and reducing numbers in the oversized army. The Catholic church is by far the most powerful institution in Spain. It has a dominant role in society, a vice-like grip on education and owns enormous amounts of property.

Within a couple of days of the revolt starting, Spain is split more or less down the middle, geographically and politically, with the vast agricultural lands of the West and South of Spain favouring the rebels. To the North and East, in the Basque Country, Catalonia, Madrid and most areas South of the capital, people's militias and army elements that remain loyal to the government are in control. These are the mostly heavily industrialised and radicalised parts of the country.

In September, Franco is formally appointed as 'Head of State' and Supreme Commander of the rebel forces. His aim is to instal in Spain a regime of *Franquismo* – an authoritarian ideology of his own composition based on medieval Catholicism, nationalism, anti-modernism and Fascism. Spain becomes a divisive issue internationally between the Left and the Right and it intersects with the wider tensions and anxieties in Europe over the rise of Hitler's Germany and the growing influence of the Soviet Union under Stalin.

In October 1936, in the city of Albacete, South of Madrid, representatives of the Comintern begin the formation of International Brigades of Communists and other progressives to come to Spain to fight with the Spanish people in defence of freedom and democracy and against dictatorship and Fascism. On 22 October, the first Brigade is formed, the 11th or Thaëlmann Brigade, mainly composed of Austrian and German volunteers. They are followed on 9 November by the French-Belgian 12th Brigade and the following day by the 13th (multinational) Brigade and the French '*La Marseillaise*' 14th Brigade. The 15th International Brigade, for English-speakers, is not formed until 31 January 1937. In all, there will be forty thousand international volunteers, including just under two hundred and fifty Irish, of whom only a quarter come directly from Ireland, half from Britain and the rest mostly from the United States and Canada.

After Mossie and his comrades arrive, they are billeted in the Castell de Figueras, the town's magnificent medieval fortress which has been an army post for many years. At the outbreak of Franco's rebellion, troops loyal to the government cornered their Francoist officers in the dungeons and killed them with hand grenades. At Figueras, there are volunteers assembled from at least twenty-four countries, including Britain, Ireland, France, Belgium, the United States, Canada, Serbia, Czechoslovakia, Poland, Italy, Germany, Japan, China, Cuba and Colombia.

After a few days in Figueras, the volunteers take a special but ramshackle train to Barcelona. They parade four abreast from the train station preceded by a military band and receive a rapturous welcome from the thousands of Catalans thronging the streets. From Barcelona, they take another train to Valencia, the seat of the Republican government since they fled from Madrid a few months earlier, and from there a slow and dreary night journey by train on to Albacete, the headquarters of the International Brigades.

There, they spend their first night in a large and gloomy former *Guardia Civil* barracks and the following day they assemble in the bull ring where they are sorted into national groups and asked about their military experience, if any. Artillery men, cavalry, telephonists, electricians, and motor mechanics are asked to step forward and identify themselves. The British and Irish volunteers are taken in open topped lorries on an hour-long journey, on poor roads, to Madrigueras, the Headquarters of the British Battalion. They arrive there in a cold and dampening drizzle, a perennial feature of Winter in this part of Spain.

Madrigueras is a poor village. The three hundred inhabitants are indentured peasants, tillers of the soil, exploited by a handful of very rich feudal landlords. The volunteers are billeted on straw mattresses in the few large houses of the village, owned by Fascist supporters who have fled. They sleep on the floors. The food is poor as is the supply of water but there is an abundance of cheap wine and there are problems with drunkenness and poor discipline. There is no tobacco to be bought in the village and the volunteers must make do with the cigarettes that arrive in parcels from home.

The volunteers are issued with strong boots, rough khaki uniforms and a tin *Adrian* helmet of the kind worn by French troops. In battle, these helmets provide little real protection and many volunteers throw them away. They are given two coarse woollen blankets and other accessories of soldiering. Training is hampered by lack of guns and the volunteers recourse to wielding wooden 'rifles' and sticks and using large wooden rattles to simulate the noise of machine gun fire. In the evenings, the political commissars give lectures on their role in the Brigades, a summary of Spanish history and an analysis of the early days of fighting in the war.

The British battalion is designated as the 57th Battalion of the Republic's Popular Army. It consists of three infantry companies and one machine gun company. Mossie is entered in the battalion records as Rifle Number 715 and is assigned to the infantry in Number 1 Company.

His political affiliations are recorded as IRA, Republican Congress and Communist Party of Ireland (and 'lapsed' Communist Party of Great Britain). A company is commanded by a lieutenant (*teniente*) and a political commissar. Each company consists of about a hundred men, divided into three sections and these, in turn, are divided into three platoons of eight or more men. A sergeant commands a platoon and a corporal is in command of a section.

On 11 December 1936, Frank Ryan and about eighty volunteers – some Communists, mostly members of the Irish Republican Army and others who are members of the Irish Republican Congress – leave Westland Row railway station in Dublin to travel to Spain. They travel by boat to Liverpool and then via London, Paris and Perpignan to the Spanish border.

Ryan is from Elton, in County Limerick and has a distinguished record with the IRA in the Irish War of Independence. He is a founding member of the Irish Republican Congress, a breakaway group from the post-Civil War IRA. Ryan, Peadar O'Donnell, George Gilmore and a few others believe that the IRA should lead a popular front of progressive forces and strive for an Irish Workers' and Small Farmers' Republic.

The Congress volunteers believe that their struggle in Ireland against General Eoin O'Duffy's Fascist Blueshirts and in favour of a socialist republic is the same as that of the supporters of the Spanish Popular Front government. Wherever democracy is under threat, these Irishmen believe the fight to defend it is their fight as well.

Ryan explains their reasoning: 'to redeem the Irish honour besmirched by the intervention of Irish Fascism on the side of the Spanish Fascist rebels... to aid the revolutionary movements in Ireland to defeat the Fascist menace at home, and ... to establish the closest bonds of friendship between the Republican democracies of Ireland and Spain.'

A few days after his arrival in Spain, at the *Commandancia* of the International Brigades in Albacete, Ryan is appointed Political Commissar of the Irish volunteers, with the rank of Captain. Most of the English-speaking volunteers in Albacete have little military training and they are assigned to the 145-strong No. 1 Company of the 12th (*Marseillaise*) Battalion, part of the 14th (*Marseillaise*) International Brigade, which is mostly comprised of French and Belgian volunteers. Forty-three of the Irish volunteers are sent to the Cordoba front as part of the 14th International Brigade, to take part in the first major battle of the war, at Lopera, in December 1936. Their brave performance under fire is impressive and seven of them are killed. Later, early in January 1937, the survivors join the defence of Madrid against Franco's major offensive on the Western and North Western sides of the city and Ryan is sent to Madrid as well. The Irish fight well in defence of the city, at Las Rozas.

When the Irish Republican Congress makes it known that their volunteers should be organised as a separate national unit – contrary to Comintern policy – Harry Pollitt, General Secretary of the Communist Party of Great Britain agrees. On New Year's Day 1937, Frank Ryan tells his Irish colleagues: 'The unit now at the front, the unit now in training and the other comrades on their way to us will be united in one unit. This unit will be part of the English-speaking Battalion which is to be formed. Irish, English, Scots and Welsh comrades will fight, side by side, against the common enemy – Fascism. It must be made clear that in the International Brigades in which we serve, there are no national differences. We are all comrades. We have all come here as soldiers of liberty to demonstrate Republican Ireland's solidarity with the gallant Spanish workers and peasants...'

Early in January 1937, Frank Ryan is assigned to work with the Italian 12th International Brigade (Garibaldi) in Madrid. Shortly after that, his stand-in, Terry Flanagan, is arrested as a political 'suspect' and is to be sent home. With these two key Irish leaders out of the way, at the British Battalion's headquarters in Madrigueras, *apparatchiks* of the Communist Party of Great Britain conspire to rid themselves of the Irish from the Battalion.

There are many reasons for this move, none of them honourable. Among some of the British officers there is an underlying patronising attitude towards the Irish that sometimes borders on racism; there are charges of stereotypical drunkenness and ill-discipline against some of the Irishmen. There is a suspicion that because a high proportion of the Irish volunteers are Republicans primarily, rather than Communists, (and are loyal to Frank Ryan) that the harsh disciplinary regime of the CPGB will not sit well with them.

Among the Irish, there is a dawning realisation that some of their British officers served in the Anglo-Irish War with the notorious and detested Black-and-Tans or the Royal Irish Constabulary Auxiliaries. The Battalion O/C, Wilf Macartney, and another officer, George Nathan, served in Ireland with the Auxiliaries. Nathan is thought to have been a member of the undercover gang who, in 1921, murdered the *Sinn Féin* Mayor of Limerick, George Clancy, and his predecessor, Michael O'Callaghan. There is some anger, too, that the British Communist Party's newspaper. '*The Daily Worker*' does not acknowledge the Irish volunteers' signal part in the fighting at Lopera.

Contrary to the Brigades' policy against encouraging national preferences, Macartney and the hard-line Political Commissar, Dave Springhall, summon a meeting of the Irish volunteers on 12 January and about forty-five of them attend. They are asked if they wish to transfer to the American Lincoln Battalion, recently arrived at their headquarters at Villanueva de la Jara, thirty kilometres to the North.

The main reason given by the speakers favouring a transfer is what they describe as the wrongs done to Ireland by the English in the past. Several volunteers, including Peter O'Connor and the Tyrone born poet, Charlie Donnelly, speak strongly against a transfer to the Lincolns, arguing for the need to distinguish British workers from their imperial ruling classes. A slim majority of the men present vote to transfer to the Americans and on 19 January, twenty-four Irishmen, mostly ex-IRA and Republican Congress members, including O'Connor, Donnelly, Frank Edwards and Johnny Power, make their way to Villanueva de la Jara. Mossie Quinlan is among those who decide to remain with their British comrades.

Shortly after the split, on 31 January, the arrival back at base of the remaining elements of No. 1 Company from the vicious battles at Lopera and Las Rozas boosts morale. Their leader, Christopher 'Kit' Conway, and their Commissar, Captain Frank Ryan forcefully raise the convening of the 'split' meeting. The Brigades' Political Commissar, André Marty, sets up an investigating commission. The commission finds that Springhall's actions and decisions were entirely incorrect and would lead to political issues. Instead, the Irish are to remain with the British battalion and those who have gone to the Americans will be regrouped with the British.

On 2 February, a compromise is announced at the Brigade HQ in Albacete. There will be a Scottish Commanding Officer appointed to the British Battalion, someone with military experience, and Frank Ryan is to be politically responsible for the Irish volunteers. The Commanding Officer of the 15th Brigade, the Hungarian Colonel János Gálicz, endorses the decision but it is never implemented because it is overtaken by the onward rush of events towards confrontation at Jarama. In the build up to Jarama, Springhall is sacked as Battalion Political Commissar and is replaced by George Aitken. Captain Tom Wintringham takes over command of the Battalion from Macartney. Frank Ryan is assigned to the important task of compiling and editing '*The Book of the XV Brigade,*

Records of British, American, Canadian and Irish Volunteers in Spain 1936-38'.

On 6 February 1937, Franco renews his attack on Madrid. His intention is to cross the river Jarama, to the Southeast of the city, and bisect the highway from Madrid to Valencia, (the Republic's temporary capital). If he succeeds, he will cut off vital supplies of food, fuel and munitions that pass along the road and considerably shorten the war.

Franco's field commander in the Jarama sector, Colonel José Enrique Varela Iglesias, commands twenty-five thousand troops, experienced elite Moroccan *regulares* of the Army of Africa or members of the Spanish Foreign Legion. They are organised into six battalions and eleven reserve battalions, with armoured and machine gun support from the Nazi German Condor Legion. By the evening of the first day of engagement, Varela Iglesias's troops have pushed the Republican forces Eastwards, back to the banks of the Jarama.

Over the next three days, the Fascists continue to press forward even though the Republican commander, General José Miaja, deploys elite forces against them – the Lister, Campesino and 11th International Brigades. During these days, the Fascists secure several crossings of the river.

Also on 6 February, after completing five weeks of training, the volunteers of the British Battalion are ordered to pack their gear and board a convoy of lorries to be transported to the railway station at Albacete. In the bull ring there, they are given Mosin-Nagant rifles – Russian Imperial Army Great War vintage - that are part of a donation to the Spanish Republic from the Leftist government of Mexico. When they get their weapon, the men sign their names in an old exercise book and are issued with a bayonet - the Mosin-Nagant is more accurate with bayonet fixed - and several packages of ammunition.

By nightfall, they are on a slow moving blacked-out train heading for Villarubbia de Santiago, a few kilometres east of Aranjuez.

In the early morning, they march into the village of Chinchon, overlooking the valley of the River Tajuna. On the far side of this valley rise the hills of the Sierra Pingarron from which comes the distant rumble of artillery and later, as the night draws in, the flashes of heavy guns may be seen.

Within a few days, they will be thrust into the insatiable, gory maw of the battle of Jarama.

Chapter Three

<u>Mossie – Family and Politics</u>

For working class people in the depressed Ireland of the 1930s London is the real economic capital and the last resort in the search for a job. Waterford, as a terminus of the Great Western Railway, has a direct physical link by rail to Paddington Station in the centre of London and the city has passenger connections to a number of British ports. It is no surprise, therefore, that at some stage in the early Thirties (possibly as early as 1932), Mossie Quinlan emigrates to London in search of work. There, he finds an active branch of the Irish Republican Congress among the emigrants and it appears that he joins the Communist Party of Great Britain.

He works as a 'commercial traveller', an obsolete occupation. His job is to solicit orders from retail outlets for the products of big manufacturers and to ensure that the shops maintain sufficient stocks of the producer's goods. It is low paid work. Most of his precarious income is derived from a percentage commission on the orders he generates, and it involves a lot of travelling in third class train carriages to dingy, provincial towns and overnight stays in small, grubby hotels or guesthouses.

Mossie is one of eleven men from Waterford who volunteer to fight in Spain to defend democracy against fascism. Some are Communists, some members of the IRA or the Irish Republican Congress, founded and led by War of Independence veterans like Frank Ryan. Some are wounded in Spain. All are brave but only Mossie is killed in action.

When he enlists, Mossie gives his Irish address as that of his grandmother, Bridget Quinlan, at 27 The Glen in Waterford. In the 1911 Census, she is recorded as living with her husband, Alderman Maurice

Quinlan, and a large family in an elegant three storey townhouse at 13 Mary Street in the city. By the 1930s, the couple are in their seventies and they may have retired to a smaller house in The Glen.

Mossie's grandfather, Alderman Maurice Quinlan, Justice of the Peace, later a Peace Commissioner, is the lynchpin of a long-tailed Quinlan clan and political dynasty in Waterford city. He is a long serving member of the Corporation and is Mayor of the city in 1906/07. He owns two butcher's shops in the city centre, a farm to fatten cattle to provide meat for his shops and he lives in a substantial town house. One of his earliest memories, from when he is only five years of age, is of being part of a crowd of several thousand people on the Hill of Ballybricken in 1864 watching the execution of Thomas Walsh, the last prisoner to be hanged in public outside Waterford Jail. Maurice's brother, James, is also an Alderman and is the city's High Sheriff for many years.

The Alderman's father, James Quinlan, is born in poor and humble circumstances in a lane off Ballybricken Fair Green, the historic location where the commercial interests of the farmers in the surrounding countryside coincide with those of the city's meat processors and inhabitants. He marries the daughter of a next-door neighbour, Margaret Caulfield, and eventually rises in the world to own a butcher's shop in nearby Barrack Street, a busy commercial street, one of the main thoroughfares in and out of the city to the West.

Ballybricken and its surrounding areas are outside the city walls – they are part of the Liberties of Waterford – and the power and wealth of British rule in the city does not sit well with its inhabitants. James Quinlan is a close personal friend and political supporter of the Waterford-born leader of the Young Ireland movement, Thomas Francis Meagher, one of the organisers of the 1848 Rising, later a Brigadier General in the Union army in the American Civil War and acting Governor of Montana. Twenty years after the Young Ireland attempt at a rising, Ballybricken is a hive of the secretive Fenians, the Irish Republican Brotherhood.

Alderman Maurice Quinlan is a staunch supporter of Home Rule for Ireland, a political ally and a close friend of Charles Stewart Parnell, the leader of the Irish Parliamentary Party.

The Irish Party splits rancorously in 1890 because of Parnell's adulterous affair with Katherine O'Shea – the wife of one of his MPs - and the leader of the minority Parnellite faction at Westminster is John Redmond. He contests Parnell's old seat in a byelection in Cork City but is defeated. In 1891, the Alderman leads a small delegation from Waterford to invite Redmond – who is seeking to re-enter Parliament -to contest a byelection in Waterford City.

In a bitter contest between the Parnellite and anti-Parnellite factions, Redmond defeats Michael Davitt, the radical advocate of tenants' rights and land reform, and establishes a symbiotic relationship with the electors of Waterford that lasts until his death in 1918. Redmond later becomes leader of the Irish Party. His greatest political achievement is when Home Rule for Ireland is enacted at Westminster in 1914, only to be deferred because of Orange/Loyalist opposition in the North-East of Ireland and the outbreak of the Great War.

Alderman Quinlan does not hesitate to break irrevocably with Redmond after the Party Leader makes a speech in county Wicklow in September 1914 advocating that young Irishmen should join the British Army to defend Ireland's shores against invasion and to fight 'wherever the firing line extends.' The Alderman withdraws his support from Redmond and the Irish Party and becomes a founder member of the Waterford City *Sinn Féin* Club. Redmond's call splits the Irish Volunteers – formed in 1913 in opposition to the Loyalist Ulster Volunteers – and the vast majority of the Executive and membership of the organisation follow Redmond into the National Volunteers, leaving only four thousand or so members remaining loyal to Eoin MacNéill, Patrick Pearse and the Irish Volunteers. The split is an important milestone in the events leading to Easter Week 1916.

Some months after the Rising, a confidential police report to Dublin Castle notes that in Waterford city, the Irish Volunteers and their associated boy scouts, *Fianna Éireann*, meet more regularly of late 'but no one in the city of any importance has joined them except some members of the Quinlan family who for some time have been estranged from Redmond.'

Alderman Quinlan and his wife have nine children – three girls and six boys. His fervent support for Parnell is reflected in the names of two of them. A daughter, born in 1893, is named Margaret Ivy (Parnell's date of death, 6 October 1891, is traditionally called 'Ivy Day') and a son, named Charles Stewart, is born in 1895. Some of the boys eventually follow their father's footsteps into the council chamber of Waterford Corporation, initially as *Sinn Féin* representatives or later as Independents – Patrick, Nicholas (the author's grandfather) and Maurice (Mossie's father).

Maurice Quinlan junior marries Eileen (Ellen) Reidy on 15 June 1910. They are both aged nineteen. A few months later, Eileen's father – Michael, (who works as a clerk in a flour merchants) dies on Christmas Eve from tuberculosis and Probate of his Will is granted to her father-in-law, Alderman Maurice Quinlan and the Mayor of Waterford, James Hackett. His estate is worth about €50,000 in present day values. So, it appears there is a close friendship or bond between the Reidy and Quinlan families.

Just nine months and two days after their wedding, their first child, Maurice Patrick, is born on Saint Patrick's Day 1911. On the Marriage Certificate, their occupations are stated as butcher and clerk, respectively, though on the Birth Certificate, the father is described as a 'cattle dealer'. Mossie is named after his father and grandfather, both named Maurice. The family live in a lodging house at 17 Terminus Road, Tramore – on the South-East coast of Ireland - not far from the railway station that, since Victorian times, links the seaside resort to Waterford City, eleven kilometres away.

When he is only sixteen days old, Mossie is recorded at 17 Terminus Road in the Census of Ireland, taken on 2 April 1911. His name is given as 'Laurence P' and he is stated to be one year old. A genealogist advises that the handwriting on the census return form appears to be that of the census enumerator, rather than Mossie's father as head of the household. Enumerator errors of this kind are common in the old Census forms and are a hazard of searching through Census records.

Other sons follow in quick order and the family practice of naming them after political heroes continues into this generation– Michael Quinlan (1913), is named after his maternal grandfather, in accordance with the custom of the time for the second born boy, but he is followed by Éamon De Valera Quinlan (1918), and the youngest, Terence Quinlan (1921), named for Terence MacSwiney, the *Sinn Féin* Lord Mayor of Cork who died in Brixton Prison in 1920 after a hunger strike lasting seventy-four days.

Mossie is thirteen years of age when tragedy strikes the young family. On 9 March 1924 Ellen dies of tuberculosis and Mossie's father is left with four young boys to care for. He remarries a woman from Carlow, named Agnes, and eventually the family settle down in a modest red brick house in South Parade, in Waterford. Neither their Marriage Certificate nor Agnes's Death Certificate is traceable but she is mentioned as his widow in his Obituary in 1959.

Mossie attends the Christian Brothers run Waterpark College most likely because it is near his home and therefore convenient. Waterpark is not a typical working class Brothers' school but is mainly for the sons of Catholic families aspiring for economic and social advancement for their sons. The school sport is rugby rather than the Gaelic games preferred in most other Christian Brothers' schools. Another Waterford International Brigader, Frank Edwards, attends the same school a few years ahead of Mossie and becomes a primary school teacher.

At the apogee of Alderman Quinlan's career, Lieutenant Thomas Cleary, of the Irish Volunteers and *Sinn Féin*, describes him as 'a strong man of the city, a man who had great powers of persuasion'. He heckles Redmond at an unruly public meeting in Waterford City Hall and the Royal Irish Constabulary remove him and his sons from the meeting.

In 1917 *Sinn Féin* calls a mass rally in Waterford. One of the organisers is my paternal grandfather, Councillor Patrick Cahill, whose trade as a butcher brings him into contact with the Quinlan family. The Constabulary ban the holding of the meeting within the city precincts. Instead, despite a huge downpour of rain, hundreds of people gather outside the city at Ballinaneeshagh and lustily cheer speeches from the platform by Alderman Quinlan, the President of *Sinn Féin*, Éamon De Valera, and the Vice President, Arthur Griffith. In his speech De Valera says, 'The best proof of the present position in this country is the presence of some of Mr. Redmond's previous strongest supporters here on my platform.'

The death of John Redmond in March 1918 is followed by one of the ugliest, most violent byelection campaigns ever seen on the island of Ireland. Redmond's son, Captain William Redmond, solicits votes wearing the uniform of the Irish Guards. His Sinn Féin opponent, Dr. Vincent White, is a popular local doctor. With other leading members of Sinn Féin, Éamon de Valera comes to Waterford to campaign and has to be rescued from a Redmondite mob by a group of Irish Volunteers. The Volunteer Hall and the Sinn Féin offices are besieged around the clock by Redmondites.

Sinn Féin and the Volunteers draft in activists from every part of the country to protect their leaders, the candidate and local election workers. Each night, election rallies are followed by riots, and police and military reinforcements are drafted in. There are further riots and pitched battles on polling day and the Sinn Féin candidate is temporarily hospitalised after being attacked on his way to vote. In later years, Vice-Commandant Thomas Brennan, of the East Waterford Brigade of the Volunteers, ruefully recalls 'I met several of these men years afterwards who had served in flying columns in Cork, Kerry and Tipperary and they all told me that they would much prefer to repeat the service they had given in the IRA columns than serve in an election campaign in Waterford.'

Alderman Quinlan and his sons – including Mossie's father – are in the thick of the campaign to elect the Sinn Féin candidate and they face the wrath of their onetime Redmondite colleagues. Dr. White is defeated and the extreme violence and the electoral result are repeated nine months later in the 1918 Imperial General election, though by a much smaller margin.

Thus, Alderman Maurice Quinlan and his sons and daughters are a family swept along in the tide of revolution in Ireland that courses all the way from Charles Stewart Parnell to John Redmond and on to *Sinn Féin,* the IRA and Éamon de Valera. In the Irish Civil War, the family splits into two factions - anti-Treaty De Valerites and pro-Treaty Michael Collins supporters. One daughter marries a Free State army officer but another marries the enthusiastically anti-Treaty editor of one of the local Waterford newspapers. Mossie's father is against the Treaty with Britain and is a resolute 'Dev' man.

So, Mossie Quinlan is of a family that evolves from Nineteenth Century physical force Irish nationalism to Home Rule to Republicanism, while his personal beliefs and instincts are radicalised through his experiences as a worker and his study of Marxism and Communism in the Waterford Workers' Study Group. These convictions lead him to membership of the IRA, the Irish Republican Congress, the Communist Parties of both Ireland and Britain and, ultimately, his brave fight and death at Jarama.

As a boy, with others of the extended Quinlan family, Mossie is a member of the Republican boy scouts, the *Fianna Éireann*. Later, he joins the IRA. In 1932, Peter O'Connor, one of his comrades, forms a Workers' Study Group that meets regularly in Coffeehouse Lane, in Waterford. Their purpose is to study the works of the Irish socialist thinker and activist, James Connolly, as well as Marx and Lenin and they are eager and diligent students. Mossie Quinlan is an active and prominent member.

Other members include Frank Edwards, Johnny Power and Jackie Hunt – all of whom later volunteer to fight in Spain - Jimmy Barry, a docker from Wellington Street, Margaret and Nora Murray, from Barrack Street, Fred O'Shea from Clashrea Place, Tom Coughlan of Morrisson's Road, Johnny Carr, Michael Barry from Green Street, Peter's father, James, and his brothers Jimmy and Francis. The Group has close links with the Revolutionary Workers' Group that, in 1933, becomes the Communist Party of Ireland. Most of the members are also in the IRA and, later, the left-wing Irish Republican Congress. Mossie joins the Republican Congress and later the Communist Party of Ireland and, while working in London, the Communist Party of Great Britain.

The following year, 1933, the De Valera government issues a Deportation Order against James Gralton, a socialist and Communist, who is providing inspiring leadership to the coal miners and small farmers in county Leitrim. The Waterford Workers' Study Group establishes itself as a support group for the Gralton Defence Committee.

In 1934, men of radical views like Peadar O'Donnell, George Gilmore and Frank Ryan are disillusioned with the exclusively militarist emphasis in IRA activities. There is no commitment to economic or social programmes in support of workers and small farmers battered by the Great Depression and by the effects of an economic war with Britain over the Irish refusal to pay further land annuities arising from the breakup of large estates. In March of that year, an IRA Convention rejects a motion calling for the establishment of a Republican Congress as an umbrella group for republicans, trade unionists, small farmers and people on the left of Fianna Fáil.

The following month, at a founding conference of the Republican Congress, O'Donnell, Gilmore and Ryan issue what becomes known as 'The Athlone Call'. They call for the establishment of a new force, a Republican Congress, to unite the Republican and Labour movements, as well as workers and small farmers in support of a radical political and social programme for the establishment of a united, independent and socialist Irish Republic. Mossie Quinlan and other members of the Waterford Workers' Study Group give the Republican Congress their complete support. In the following six months, there is more political and socialist agitation in Waterford than there has ever been, including a campaign against the pestilence of slum landlords.

In June 1934, eight IRA members from Waterford cycle the one hundred and forty kilometres or so to Bodenstown, county Kildare, for the annual commemoration honouring Theobald Wolfe Tone, the Father of Irish Republicanism. A small group of Protestant workers from the Shankill Road, in Belfast, take part in the parade carrying Republican Congress banners *'Wolfe Tone Commemoration 1934 – Shankill Road, Belfast Branch – Break the Connection with Capitalism'* and *'James Connolly Club Belfast – United Irishmen of 1934'*.

As they move forward towards Tone's grave, IRA elements, possibly acting on orders from higher up in the organisation, attack them and prevent them from laying a wreath. Disillusioned by this turn of events, the Waterford men resign from the IRA and are more convinced than ever that concentration on the military dimension only, to the exclusion of revolutionary politics, is a disastrous and divisive strategy.

The Waterford members of the Republican Congress are active on the industrial front as well. In August and September, they support a strike by building workers and some of them are prosecuted for unlawful assembly and assaulting members of the *Garda Síochána* while trying to prevent a scab worker moving materials from a builder's yard. After five weeks, the strike ends in partial victory for the workers.

Frank Edwards, a member of the Study Group, is the chief organiser of the Republican Congress in Waterford city and the surrounding district. He is a teacher in Mount Sion Christian Brothers' school and is sacked because he will not resign from the Congress. On 12 January 1935, a massive public protest meeting is held in Waterford, despite the Bishop's warning – read out at all the Masses in his diocese - that anyone who attends will commit a mortal sin. Opening the meeting, the Chairperson's riposte, *'We will worship God on the hillsides in spite of the priests and the devil'*, evokes rapturous applause and cheers. When Edwards arrives back from Spain, wounded, he lives in Dublin. The Archbishop of Dublin, Edward Byrne, writes to him telling him that he will not be employed in any Catholic school. Instead, Edwards is fortunate to get work teaching in a Jewish school in Dublin.

The Waterford branch sends eight delegates to the conference of the Republican Congress in the Town Hall, Rathmines, in September 1934. The conference is split between those, like Peadar O'Donnell, who favour the formation of a broad, popular front of republicans and socialists, workers and small farmers, Protestants and Catholics and others who prefer the formation of a political party to fight for a Workers' Republic.

The Waterford delegates support O'Donnell's Resolution No. 2, which prevails, but the defeated delegates withdraw from the conference, leave the Congress and by 1936 the organisation is in terminal decline. Its unquenchable legacy is the courage shown in Spain later that year and subsequently by its leader, Frank Ryan, and by members like Mossie Quinlan.

Chapter Four

<u>Remembering Mossie</u>

Mossie Quinlan is one of five Waterford men who fought at Jarama. Their names are Paddy Power and Peter O'Connor, Mossie - killed in action - and Jackie Hunt and Johnny Power who are wounded. Mossie is buried in the cemetery at Morata de Tajuna, the nearest town to the battlefield.

In time, the victorious Fascists desecrate his and the other graves and pile the remains on a rubbish dump in a corner of the cemetery. Years later, a Frenchman, François Mazou, who was a political commissar in Spain and was wounded at Jarama – with the help of some gravediggers – locates the rubbish pit where the remains are dumped under broken pots, dead flowers and assorted junk at the edge of the cemetery. In Dublin, the *Brigadista* veteran Bob Doyle and Harry Owens lobby the government to help have this wrong rectified. Then, in better times in Spain, in 1994 a Socialist Prime Minister, Felipe González, accedes to a request from a Socialist Irish Minister for Foreign Affairs, Dick Spring, to respectfully re-inter the remains of five thousand Spanish militia members and International Brigaders in a communal grave.

On a marble slab, set into the wall, in gold letters, are these words in Spanish:

'To the memory of the fallen heroes of Jarama who made the supreme sacrifice in the defence of Madrid and succeeded in keeping open the road to Valencia. 1936-39. No Pasaran!'

At the dedication ceremony, Peter O'Connor stands near his pal's last resting place. As the only remaining Irish survivor of Jarama, He speaks on behalf of the Irish Brigaders present:

'To be here today brings back vivid memories of those days in 1937 when the gallant Army of Spain, ably assisted by the International Brigade, kept the road open to Madrid.

I was twenty-four years old when I fought here in Jarama. When the vile creed of fascism is again raising its ugly head, it is vital for the young people of today to learn the lesson taught in Spain – the lesson of unity. We need that unity more than ever today when fascism is on the rise all over the world, even in Germany. We must again say 'Never!' to racism and fascism. *No Pasaran! Salud!*'

Spain's final tribute to the International Brigaders comes two years later when the *Cortes Generales*, the Spanish parliament, votes to confer citizenship on the surviving veterans of the Brigades. The conferring ceremony takes place in November 1996 and the Irish delegation is led by Michael O'Riordan, veteran of the Battle of the Ebro in July 1938, wounded at Hill 481 and former General Secretary of the Communist Party of Ireland. The conferring fulfils the commitment made in 1938 by Juan Negrin, Prime Minister of the Spanish Republic, and expressed exquisitely at the Brigades' standing down parade in Barcelona by Dolores Ibarruri, the charismatic Communist leader known as '*La Pasionaria*': 'We shall not forget you... Come back to us and here you will find a homeland,'

In Ireland, Mossie and his comrades are remembered and honoured by the Communist Party and some of the trade unions. His death is also noted in an unexpected place. Among the memorabilia decorating Johnny Fox's tourist pub, in the Dublin mountains, is a framed copy of page one of the 'Irish Press' of Saturday, 20 March 1937 reporting his death and that of Jim Foley.

In 2004, the city of Waterford unveils a memorial - an eight-tonne block of Spanish granite - carved by the Wexford sculptor, Michael

Warren. The only photograph of Mossie that I have ever seen is in the commemoration booklet for that event. In a grainy black-and-white image, he is with five companions and all of them are wearing the type of heavy, double-breasted, belted overcoat that was fashionable among young men up to the Fifties. They are seated at the old bridge across the River Suir in Waterford, ironically the bridge for which his grandfather signed the construction contract as Mayor. Mossie is wearing a trilby hat at a jaunty angle, his hands rest nonchalantly on his thighs and he has a cigarette dangling from his mouth. He is looking confidently – almost defiantly – at the camera, and I wonder if, beneath his hat, he has the same golden red hair as his father.

Survivors fare better in memory and history. They are around to speak of what they did, if they choose. Those who keep diaries or write books or memoirs maintain their place more easily in memory. Mossie never returned and with only a few exceptions, his family shunned his memory, at least publicly.

At the age of nineteen, his brother, Éamon, emigrated to England in 1937 and soon after joined the British Army. His family recall that he looked up to and admired his eldest brother and they remember him as a kind and gentle man. Like many young Irish people, his primary reason for emigrating may have been to get work or simply to get away from home. However, the Army was never more than a mere job for him and he was conscious of the real and looming threat of Fascism emanating from Europe – the German remilitarisation of the Rhineland and Mussolini's conquest of Abyssinia.

That he emigrated in the year Mossie was killed, and at such a young age, and then went on to fight to defeat Fascism, might suggest that he was in some way mindful of his brother's sacrifice. Éamon served throughout the war and attained the rank of Staff Sergeant. He commanded a group of men during the 1940 evacuation from Dunkirk and saw service in France and Germany – possibly Belgium or the Netherlands as well – and he was part of the Allied occupation occupation forces in Germany at the end of the war. He took a piece of shrapnel in the white of his eye but otherwise escaped physical injury. Éamon named his first three boys after his brothers – Michael, Terence and Maurice Philip.

Mossie's youngest brother, Terence, remained steadfastly loyal to his memory. He began his working life as a clerk in the General Post Office, in Waterford, and eventually became a highly respected General Secretary of the Postal and Telecommunications Workers' Union and a member of the Executive Council of the Irish Congress of Trade Unions. Terence was a tireless advocate and campaigner for equal pay and equal rights for women and an implacable opponent of apartheid South Africa, long before these positions became mainstream in the trade union movement.

In 1986, he was the opening chairperson at a seven-hour long event in Dublin to commemorate the Irish volunteers who died with the International Brigades. He said then that 'those who went from Ireland to fight with the International Brigade were disgracefully propagandised against. My own brother was killed in the battle of Jarama and I know what kind of man he was, as well as the others who went from his native Waterford. The time to honour them is well overdue.' Two years after that event, the PTWU chartered a plane to fly old comrades to Barcelona to attend the ceremonies commemorating the fiftieth anniversary of the standing down parade of the International Brigades and Terence Quinlan was among the group who travelled.

Other returned veterans were spurned and victimised publicly but their families honoured them and they had children and grandchildren who actively kept the flame of memory burning brightly. A few of the Quinlan family, who followed the pro-Treaty Collins and Griffith in the Civil War and then supported the Irish Free State, had become Blueshirts by 1936 and Mossie's role in Spain did not suit their political narrative.

In October 2016, the President of Ireland, Michael D Higgins, spoke to the Annual General Meeting of the International Brigade Memorial Trust in Liberty Hall, in Dublin. He recalled that, eighty years earlier, a group of activists had gathered in the same location, bound by ties of idealism, solidarity, internationalism and, above all, courage, before becoming volunteers in the International Brigade. Citing the death of the young Irish poet, Charlie Donnelly, at Jarama, the President had this to say about the unresolved conflict felt by many families of the fallen in Spain:

'Ten days after his death, Charles Donnelly's body, - 'face fresh, naive looking' - was buried beneath one of those olive trees in that foreign land far away from his native Tyrone; his family left unaware of his death for some time, his distressed father unable to talk about him for years... The silence of the relatives of the lost is as moving now to recall as it was understandable in its time.

Sadly, such silence was not unusual. Many of those who died so bravely for freedom, were marginalised back home in Ireland for many years. Many had their teaching posts taken from them. Communist Party spokesperson, Eugene McCartan[3], describing the anguish and despair of those who lost sons to anti-fascist forces in the Spanish Civil War said:

'To be attached to someone who died was not safe in Ireland. The Catholic church made a rallying cry for Fascists and held collections to support Franco. It was no wonder families kept their heads down.'

These remarks underline some of the reasons why Mossie Quinlan remained so elusive for so long.

In his mid-twenties, why was he willing to fight and die far from home for a cause that was advanced in slogans about Democracy, Republicanism and the death of Fascism? Was it what we call courage

---

[3] General Secretary, Communist Party of Ireland

or just foolhardiness? When the order comes and there is that great rush forward towards the enemy, is it cowardice that keeps us moving forward because we lack the courage to turn around and go back?

I think there was more to it than that. In his memoir about his time in Spain, Mossie's friend Peter O'Connor wrote 'You have to believe in something – in a cause that will make the world a better place, or you have wasted your life.' Mossie was an idealist. Clearly, he believed in something - call it Communism, Republicanism or Democracy and, unlike most of us, he was prepared to fight and die for what he believed in.

His story is one that tells of the fragilities of memory and of how heroes may live on in some way but their deaths can leave tragedy behind them.

We should remember but never judge.

Chapter Five

<u>My Search Begins</u>

As a child in the company of adults, it is often at the moments when they glance in your direction, and then lower their voices, that you listen most intently. Their act of attempted concealment heightens your childish curiosity. These are the snatched comments that you recall most vividly years later. In my case, none more so than the short, subdued conversations of my childhood that ended often with a sigh and a comment like 'Ah, poor Mossie...'

Of Mossie Quinlan there was the little bit that I knew myself. Then, there was what I heard from other people, and, finally, there was the sparse amount written about him in official records and books. I knew that he fought in the Spanish Civil War as a member of the British battalion of the 15th International Brigade and that he was killed in action in a battle near the River Jarama, just outside Madrid, sometime in the third week of February 1937. All in all, I knew very little but, eighty years after his death, I began a journey to find out more.

He was my mother's first cousin. In the formal way that these things are described, I am therefore his 'first cousin, once removed' or, more informally, his second cousin. For more than seventy years after his death he was hardly ever mentioned in our family and then only in those hushed voices that I overheard as a child. In holy, Catholic Ireland of the 1930s it may have been because of shame, because he had fought in Spain with the Reds who, they were constantly told by newspapers and pulpits, had killed priests, raped nuns and burned churches.

The family lived at a number of addresses in Waterford before settling down at 34, South Parade. The houses there were built around

1830, at the southern end of the city. The street is bounded at one end by the magnificent People's Park and at the other by the busy, commercial thoroughfare of Johnstown.

The houses have a pleasant red brick frontage. Towards the Park end, they are tall, bow fronted, with granite steps leading up to elegant doors and fanlights. These were the dwellings of wealthy merchants and the professional classes, many of them Protestants or Quakers. Towards the other end, however, the houses are more modest – the homes of artisans and tradesmen. It was in one of these smaller houses that Mossie's family settled down. His father was self-employed, variously described in official records and trade directories as a butcher, a victualler or a cattle dealer. In the days before livestock marts, the earnings were fairly good and the family was probably reasonably well off.

When I was a child in the 1950s, Mossie's father was a frequent visitor to our home and, sometimes, I visited their house in South Parade with my mother. By that time, Maurice - the father - was in his sixties. A typical Quinlan man in appearance, he was tall and broadly built. Like the people of the Pacific Kingdom of Tonga – the most obese population in the world - the Quinlans seemed to regard being overweight or obese as a badge of wealth and strength. I suppose it may have been some sort of a distinction at a time when many other people were poor and could not afford a proper diet.

My first encounters with him were when I was six or seven years old and only twenty years after his son's death in Spain. I imagine the memories were still fresh and there must have been an aching hurt. When Maurice senior was a young man he had reddish, golden hair and his nickname in the family was 'The Golden Lamb'. By the time he entered my life, his hair had gone white, he wore horn rimmed glasses and his nickname had been changed – affectionately, I think – to 'The Big Slob'. I think the physical change may have reflected the deterioration in his demeanour in the years since Mossie's death.

In our tiny kitchen, he sat in an armchair beneath a big picture of the Sacred Heart with a flickering red votive lamp in front of it. He was dressed like a typical cattle dealer.

He wore a dark grey three-piece suit, big black laced boots with a couple of loops of the laces secured around the top, a heavy brown overcoat and a soft hat. All he was missing was the symbol of his occupation, a stout ash plant to drive cattle. Often, he kept his overcoat on when he sat down even though the fire was lit and was throwing out heat.

We never spoke much to each other, that I can recall. He never seemed happy in himself and spent most of the time hunched over the fire, gazing into the flames or watching the coals reddening. Sometimes, he leaned his arm on the mantelpiece where there was a signed photograph of Father Patrick Peyton, the Irish American Rosary Crusade priest, a statue of the Peruvian-born Dominican brother, Martin de Porres - whose elevation to sainthood was yet to come and who was still only 'Blessed' - and a picture of my brother, Pat, who died at the age of ten.

From my mother's reaction to Pat's death, I have a real sense of how heart breaking it is for a parent to lose a child in death and that it is a burden carried throughout their life. How much harder it must have been to lose your firstborn son, named after you, in a battle in a faraway land and for a cause that you, at best, did not understand or, at worst, made you feel ashamed?

Aside from any conversation that took place with my mother, the main attraction in visiting us seemed to be that she was expert in the local cuisine that was a feature of Waterford life for generations. Both rich and poor people regularly consumed dishes concocted from almost every part of the pig, from the snout to the tail – head, feet, back bones, ribs, tail – as well as the flesh from the sides, back and belly made into rashers or sausages. All these parts were soaked in brine for long periods and were highly salted.

The rashers and sausages were fried on a pan in fat but the other bits were boiled, together with cabbage and potatoes. It was a very unhealthy diet but, as the old people used to say, 'It did us no harm'.

Being from Carlow, Maurice's second wife was not well versed in these culinary arts and, so, he visited us for a treat when the longing came over him and became too much for him to bear and, maybe, just for a few hours of respite and reflection.

Illustrations

Mossie Quinlan (on the right of photo) with friends on the city side of the bridge over the River Suir, in Waterford, sometime in the 1930s. Second from the left is Bobby Clancy, a member of the IRA. During the Second World War, the De Valera government interned Bobby and other IRA members. He died in the Curragh Military Hospital on 12 June 1941.

Mossie's grandfather, Alderman Maurice Quinlan, outside one of two butcher's shops he owned in George's Street, Waterford, with his sons John and Maurice (Mossie's father). *Photo Credit: Mossy Quinlan and Bernie Lara Quinlan*

Mossie's grandfather, Alderman Maurice Quinlan, was Mayor of Waterford in 1906/07. *(Family photograph)*

On the platform at a rally in Waterford in 1917, the President of *Sinn Féin*, Eamon de Valera, with Mossie's grandfather, Alderman Maurice Quinlan. The authorities had banned the meeting and it was held on a rural road just outside the city limits. *(Family Photograph)*

Cover of a notebook, compiled at Albacete, containing an alphabetical list of the members of the British Battalion. *RGASPI Archives 545/6/91/1*

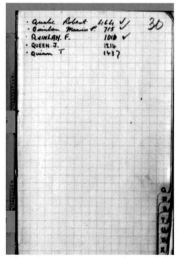

Extract from a notebook containing an alphabetical list of the members of the British Battalion, compiled at Albacete. Under the letter 'Q', Maurice P Quinlan is assigned no. 715. 'F Quinlan 1016' is Frank Quinlan, a Communist London building worker, who is not counted as an Irish volunteer though his surname indicates Irish antecedents. In June 1937, he died in a drowning accident at Mondejar. *RGASPI Archives 545/6/91/30*

Cover of the Register of members of the British Battalion, 15th International Brigade. *RGASPI Archives 545/6/91/43*

713	Murray	Ben	Irish	CP	32	40	salesman	cavalry	Sgt.	11·2·37
714	O'Sullivan	Pat.	"	CPI	6/36	22	terazzo layer	ifty		11·2·37
715	Quinlan	Maurice Pat (albert)	"	"	"	25	salesman.	ifty + artly		11·2·37
716	Russell	Jock	Brit.	CP	32	32	mechanic	ifty		11·2·37

Extract from the Register of the British Battalion. Mossie Quinlan is entry no. 715. Political affiliation – CPI (Communist Party of Ireland) since June 1936; age 25, assigned to infantry/artillery. *RGASPI Archives 545/6/91/89.*

713		21 Winchester Ave., London, N.W.6		S.		I.C.W.O...			
714		L O'Bnaghan 54 Connolly Avenue, Dublin.		S	V	ITGWU -1935-37 James Larkin W.of Dublin Br.			
						South body Dublin Br. C.P.I.			
715	grandmother 24 The Glen, Waterford, Ireland			S.		lapsed. C.P.			
	Mother	18 EdiNo. Place, Easter Rd, Edinburgh Scot.		S		Willesden Br. L.P.			

Extract from the Register of the British Battalion. Mossie's next-of-kin given as his grandmother (Bridget Quinlan) and her address as 27 The Glen, Waterford. Described as 'lapsed CP' (probably a reference to membership of the Communist Party of Great Britain) *RGASPI Archives 545/6/91/89*

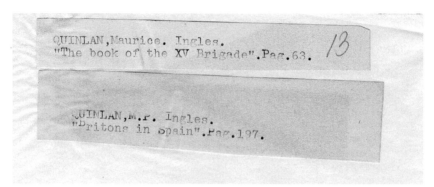

References to Mossie Quinlan in the Personnel Files of the 15th International Brigade. They refer to two books on the Brigades where he is mentioned. *RGASPI Archives 545/6/189/13/*

The first Mossie's family knew of his death in Spain was when they read about it in the Dublin newspapers on 20 March 1937, a little over a month after he was killed.

The Jarama River, looking Eastwards towards the ridge defended by the British Battalion.

The olive groves of Jarama, looking Westwards towards the river. *Photo Credit: Ger McCloskey/ David Convery*

The Conical Hill, the furthest point of advance by Mossie Quinlan's No. 1 Company, commanded by the brave and battle-experienced Tipperary man, Christopher 'Kit' Conway. *Photo Credit: Ger McCloskey/David Convery*

The view of the Jarama valley as observed by Harold Fry and the machine gunners of No. 4 Company. *Photo Credit: Ger McCloskey/David Convery*

Looking Northwards from Jarama, with Madrid visible in the distance. *Photo Credit: Ger McCloskey/David Convery*

The Sunken Road. *Photo Credit: Ger McCloskey/David Convery*

The Cookhouse, as it is today. *Photo Credit: Ger McCloskey/David Convery*

Some of Mossie Quinlan's comrades from the No. 1 Company of the British Battalion. In the middle row, second from the right, is André Diamant, the brave and resourceful Egyptian, who took over command of the Company on the first day of battle and led them through to the end.

Captain Tom Wintringham, Commanding Officer of the British Battalion at the commencement of the battle. He was wounded on the second day of fighting and his military experience and training made him a highly competent leader.

Captain Frank Ryan, veteran of the Irish War of Independence and Civil War, founder and leader of the Irish Republican Congress, and Political Commissar of the Irish volunteers in Spain. Together with Jock Cunningham, he led the Great Rally that turned the battle in the Republic's favour on 14 February 1937. *Photo provided by Seán Kelly*

The April 1937 Memorial to the fallen of Jarama.

Claire Rol-Tanguy, daughter of Colonel Henri Rol-Tanguy (Political Commissar of the 14th International Brigade) - who led the liberation of Paris in 1944 - lays flowers at the memorial marking the communal grave of International Brigaders in the cemetery at Morata de Tajuna. Mossie Quinlan is buried there.

Appendix One

Mossie Quinlan's Days in Spain

1936

1 December

Mossie Quinlan arrives in Spain from London.

1937

7 January

The first American contingent of ninety-six volunteers (all Communists) arrive at their base, Villanueva de la Jara.

12 January

At a controversial meeting at the British Battalion's training base in Madrigueras, a small majority of Irish volunteers vote to transfer the American Lincoln Battalion. Mossie and others decide to stay with the British battalion.

19 January

Twenty-four Irishmen transfer to the Lincoln Battalion in Villanueva de la Jara.

31 January

Kit Conway and other Irish Brigaders return from the Cordoba front and Conway and Frank Ryan raise the split with Peter Kerrigan, Political Commissar of the Madrigueras base. The International Brigades' Political Commissar, André Marty, sets up a commission to investigate.

2 February

A compromise is announced in Albacete. The British Battalion will have a Scottish Commanding Officer with military experience. This is never implemented because of the rush of preparation for Jarama.

George Aitken replaces Dave Springhall as Political Commissar and Captain Tom Wintringham replaces Wilf Macartney as Battalion Commanding Officer.

6 February Saturday

In heavy rain, Franco orders the commencement of the Fascist advance towards the Jarama River to cut the highway between Madrid and Valencia, where the Republican government has relocated.

7 February Sunday

The British Battalion leaves its base at Madrigueras at 10 am for La Gineta to begin their journey to the front, at Jarama. They travel by train from La Gineta to Albacete, the headquarters of the International Brigades, then on by train to Chinchon, sixteen kilometres from the Jarama River. They arrive there in darkness.

9 February Tuesday

Republican militias and the 11th and 12th International Brigades halt four advancing Fascist columns on the West bank of the Jarama.

10 February Wednesday

The heavy rain stops at Jarama.

12 February Friday

At dawn, Moroccan troops capture the San Martin bridge over the Jarama. Lieutenant-Colonel's Asensio Cabinallas's 4th Brigade are ready to cross the river - the 7th regiment to the North, the 8th to the South, where eventually they encounter the British Battalion.

In the early hours of the morning, the British Battalion transfers by truck from Chinchon into battle positions West of the town of Morata de Tajuna.

7 am The men eat breakfast.

10 am The Battalion's three rifle companies and the machine gun company move off Westwards in the direction of the Jarama River, towards a steep slope. Harold Fry discovers that his Company has the wrong calibre of bullets for their Maxim machine guns.

The Brigaders move forward to a sunken road and begin a descent into the river valley.

10.30 am Fascist bombers fly overhead to bomb the Republican base at Morata de Tajuna. Russian fighters respond, scatter the bombers and attack the Fascist positions.

1 pm Fry's machine gun crews reach their designated position on the ridge, with a commanding view of the river valley. Three Republican bombers attack Suicide Hill. Around the same time, Kit Conway orders No.1 Company back to the summit of the Conical Hill to give a better line of fire against the advancing Fascists. Fascist artillery opens fire on No. 4 Company on Suicide Hill. There are many casualties and in the confusion the Company Commander, Bert Overton, flees.

2.30 pm Mossie's Company Commander, Kit Conway, is fatally wounded.

3 pm The correct ammunition is located for No. 2 Company's Maxim machine guns and they are hauled into a commanding position.

Late afternoon Fifty Fascist machine guns are trained and firing on the Internationals' positions. They are forced to retreat to the olive groves above the valley.

6 pm The sun is setting. The Moroccans and Foreign Legionaries begin to advance from Suicide Hill. Harold Fry's Maxims, loaded with the correct ammunition, are readied and awaiting the enemy. Many Fascist troops are slaughtered before the others are driven back to Suicide Hill and the Conical Hill.

7 pm André Diamant leads a large group of No. 1 and No. 4 Companies back to the Sunken Road and they are joined there by the remnants of No. 3 Company.

At the beginning of the day, the British Battalion had deployed four hundred riflemen into battle. Now, under the darkness, a hundred of them lie dead and a hundred and forty-five are wounded.

13 February Saturday

2 am André Diamant and Fred Copeman return to the Sunken Road with about thirty stragglers rounded up at the Cookhouse.

3 am The Battalion stands to. George Aitken arrives with supplies and plenty of hot sweet coffee and thick bully beef sandwiches.

The various Companies take up their allotted positions and Wintringham sets up his HQ near the Sunken Road.

Dawn Moroccan troops attack but are beaten back by machine gun fire.

10.30 am Fascist bombers fly overhead on their way to bomb the nearby Republican-held town of Morata de Tajuna. Russian bombers fly over and their fighter escorts strafe the Fascist lines.

1 pm Three Republican bombers attack Suicide Hill where the White House is located.

2 pm A Russian T26 tank chases enemy troops on the plateau above the river valley.

Wintringham orders Aitken to lead a feint attack to the left of Suicide Hill to draw fire away from the Northern direction where the Fascists are exerting pressure on the Dimitrovs and the Franco-Belges and a gap is opening up in the front line.

3 pm Wintringham ignores an order from Colonel Gálicz to advance because he does not have the required numbers of men, tanks, artillery and air support.

4 pm Wintringham orders Aitken to withdraw back to the Sunken Road, beginning at 5 pm. He gives a similar order to Diamant and the No. 1 Company on his left flank, but to begin at 5.30 pm.

Wintringham is not aware that accurate artillery fire has rained down on Overton's No. 4 company who are between Fry's No. 2 (Machine Gun) company and Fascist troops who are advancing in the dead land to the right of their position.

4.30 pm Fry sends a runner to Wintringham to tell him that they have observed the Fascist commander in position on the front, seemingly preparing to attack. Wintringham (unaware of the defection of No. 4 Company) is satisfied that he has his men in place to hold the line.

Fascist troops get near the tired and confused gunners of No. 2 Company, overrun their machine gun position and turn the lethal guns on the British volunteers below them on the slope.

5 pm The Fascist artillery goes silent and they launch a fierce attack. Wintringham is wounded and George Aitken takes over command of the Battalion.

5.45 pm Aitken gets twelve volunteers to secure his right flank. The panic-stricken men in the Sunken Road are joined by the crew of the sole Maxim remaining in British hands. They await the next onslaught.

Darkness The firing dies down. A Fascist flare destroys the Battalion's ammunition store.

Dusk to Midnight From his sickbed in Chinchon, Jock Cunningham, the original commander of No. 1 Company, arrives at the Cookhouse behind the British positions, leading about sixty fleeing troops back to the front line.

14 February, Sunday

Cunningham begins the day by leading a successful charge to recapture some of No. 4 Company's captured machine guns.

The Battalion is just over two hundred strong.

9 am Cunningham re-occupies the Sunken Road and the Battalion spends the morning improving their defences. They are reinforced by three hundred seasoned Spanish troops from the Lister Battalion, plus experienced reinforcements from Morata de Tajuna.

Early afternoon The Fascist artillery opens up and the enemy advances in strength to the South of the Sunken Road, using captured Russian tanks. Thousands of Moroccan infantry are covered by Nazi machine gunners and planes. In a terrifying slaughter, the British flank breaks amid panic.

André Diamant leads No. 1 Company in a well-executed rear-guard action.

4.30 pm No. 1 Company dig in at their final position but then have to withdraw. Nothing stands now between the Fascists and the Madrid/ Valencia Road.

Frank Ryan imposes order on the men at the Cookhouse. Cunningham is also organising troops. They join forces, mustering a hundred and forty men, and march Westwards.

As the sun sets The Great Rally at Jarama begins.

They sing *'The Internationale'* as they march and their numbers swell. On the way, they encounter the Brigade Commander, Gálicz, and respond to his appeal to plug the gap in the line.

Dusk The Internationals emerge several hundred metres behind the Fascist line. They catch them unawares and fierce, chaotic fighting ensures. They regain the abandoned Republican lines.

Dawn The Republican counterattack has succeeded. The line is held and the Madrid to Valencia Road is secure.

15 February

The American Lincoln Battalion leave their base at Villanueva de la Jara for the front line at Jarama.

16 February

The Americans arrive at Jarama. In their ranks, Peter O'Connor spots Mossie Quinlan marching along the road with a British contingent.

17 February

A sniper kills Mossie Quinlan as he tries to rescue a wounded comrade from between the opposing lines.

18 February

Peter O'Connor hears of Mossie's death.

23 February

Spanish Republican troops attack Pingarron Hill and the river crossing outside San Martin but are repulsed by Moroccans. In the same attack, the Americans suffer severe casualties.

27 February

An attack by the Lincoln Battalion results in another horrendous slaughter of men.

A stalemate sets in, that lasts until the end of the war.

14 March

Jock Cunningham is wounded. He is promoted to the rank of Major and assigned to a Staff role in Brigade Command.

23 March

George Aitken is promoted to Brigade Commissar of the 15th International Brigade.

27 April

The former Commander of No. 4 Company, Bert Overton, is court martialled and sentenced to a labour battalion, a fate that leads to his death in the Battle of Brunete while carrying ammunition to a forward position.

29 April

The new Battalion Commanding Officer, Fred Copeman, and the Brigade Commissar, George Aitken, dedicate a battlefield memorial to the dead of Jarama.

The dead of Jarama comprise twenty thousand Fascists and twenty-five thousand Republicans. Of the five hundred British and Irish volunteers who advanced into battle on 12 February, one hundred and fifty are dead and a similar number are wounded.

Appendix Two

Frank Ryan's description of the Great Rally at Jarama on Sunday, 14 February 1937

On the road from Chinchon to Madrid, the road along which we had marched to the attack three days before, were now scattered all who survived - a few hundred Britons, Irish and Spaniards. Dispirited by heavy casualties, by defeat, by lack of food, worn out by three days of gruelling fighting, our men appeared to have reached the end of their resistance.

Some were still straggling down the slopes from what had been, up to an hour ago, the front line. And now, there was no line, nothing between the Madrid to Valencia Road and the Fascists but disorganised groups of weary, war-wrecked men. After three days of terrific struggle, the superior numbers, the superior armament of the Fascists had routed them. All, as they came back, had similar stories to tell - of comrades dead, of conditions that were more than flesh and blood could stand, of weariness they found hard to resist.

I recognised the young Commissar of the Spanish Company. His hand bloody where a bullet had grazed the palm, he was fumbling nevertheless with his automatic, in turn threatening and pleading with his men. I got Manuel to calm him, and to tell him we would rally everybody in a moment. As I walked along the road to see how many men we had, I found myself deciding that we should go back up the line of the road to San Martin de la Vega and take the Moroccans on their left flank.

Groups were lying about on the roadside, hungrily eating oranges that had been thrown to them by a passing lorry. This was no time to sort them into units. I noted with satisfaction that some had brought down spare rifles. I found my eyes straying always to the hills we had vacated. I hitched a rifle on my shoulder.

They stumbled to their feet. No time for barrack-square drill. One line of four. 'Fall in behind us'. A few were still on the grass bank beside the road, adjusting helmets and rifles.

'Hurry up!' came the cry to the ranks. Up the road towards the Cookhouse I saw Jock Cunningham assembling another crowd. We hurried up, joined forces. Together we two marched at the head. Whatever popular writers may say, neither your Briton nor your Irishman is an exuberant type. Demonstrativeness is not his dominating trait. The crowd behind us was marching silently. The thoughts in their minds could not be inspiring ones. I remembered a trick of the old days when we were holding banned demonstrations. I jerked my head back: 'Sing up, ye sons o' guns!'.

Quaveringly at first, then more lustily, then in one resounding chant the song rose from the ranks. Bent backs straightened: tired legs thumped sturdily; what had been a routed rabble marched to battle again as proudly as they had done three days before. And the valley resounded to their singing:

'Then comrades, come rally,

And the last fight let us face;

The Internationale

Unites the human race'.

On we marched, back up the road, nearer and nearer to the front. Stragglers still in retreat down the slopes stopped in amazement, changed direction and ran to join us; men lying exhausted on the roadside jumped up, cheered, and joined the ranks. I looked back. Beneath the forest of upraised fists, what a strange band! Unshaven, unkempt; bloodstained, grimy. But, full of fight again, and marching on the road back.

Beside the road stood our Brigade Commander, General Gal. We had quitted; he had stood his ground. Was it that, or fear of his reprimands, that made us give three cheers for him? Briefly, tersely, he spoke to us. We had one and a half hours of daylight in which to recapture our lost positions. 'That gap on our right?' A Spanish Battalion was coming up with us to occupy it.

Again the *'Internationale'* arose. It was being sung in French too. Our column had swelled in size during the halt; a group of Franco-Belge had joined us. We passed the Spanish Battalion.

They caught the infection; they were singing too as they deployed to the right. Jock Cunningham seemed to be the only man who was not singing. Hands thrust into his great-coat pockets, he trudged along at the head of his men. We were singing; he was planning.

As the olive groves loom in sight, we deploy to the left. At last, we are on the ridge, the ridge which we must never again desert. For while we hold the ridge, the Madrid-Valencia Road is free.

And thus, the men who had been broken and routed a few hours before, settled down for the night on the ground they had reconquered. They had dashed Fascist hopes, smashed Fascist plans. Thence forward, for more than four months, they were to fight, and many of them to die, in these olive groves. But never again were the Fascists to rout them. They were to hold that line, and save Madrid, fighting in the dauntless spirit of the great rally of that afternoon, fighting too, in the spirit of those reckless roars of laughter that night in the Wood of Death.

Appendix Three

Tom Wintringham Recalls Comrades of Jarama

The name of Jarama means, to most of us who came back from Spain, the long and dreary weeks of trench warfare among the stripped olive trees of that valley, where the British Battalion spent three months in the line without relief. And to some it means the unsuccessful attacks carried out, during the earlier months of this trench warfare, the attempts to take Pingarron Hill.

Those months of fighting made the word Jarama mean something to us that is embodied in the words of our song: It is the valley in which 'we wait patiently'. And those months were considered as a military job of work, almost as important as anything else that the Battalion did. The Spanish army was learning how to be dangerous in attack, and we made some of the experiments.

But the first days of the Jarama Battle included the severest fighting and had a greater political and military importance than has been realised by many people. If we had failed in those first days to hold our ground, under conditions more difficult and dangerous than any the Battalion met until the counterattack at Brunete, the last road into Madrid would have been cut and the great city would have been surrounded.

That would have meant the loss of Madrid two years before its eventual surrender. And such a loss of Madrid might have meant the present world war would have reached us perhaps two years earlier.

But when we piled out of our lorries at the farm cookhouse on the Chinchon road, early on the morning of 12 February 1937, we knew little of all this; the main thing we knew was that the British Battalion was going into action for the first time.

And when we had begun moving up and a 'dog-fight' of planes swung over us, many of us were changed suddenly from spectators, or men marching as they had marched in demonstrations and in peace, to soldiers, men marching with weapons and a purpose more commanding than that of any peace-time march.

Whoever remembers Jarama is likely to remember the moment they crossed for the first time the sunken road, that later was our rallying point; coming out on the crest of the hill, they saw in front of them the grass valley and the slopes that most of us called 'Suicide Hill'. Some, like myself, may have seen beyond those slopes the first parties of the Moroccans spreading out for their attack.

Many of the men who held Suicide Hill through almost all that grilling day did not realize why it was necessary for them to stay there, with their twenty-year-old, almost useless colts and 'Shoshers', without adequate support, and with crossfire striking them from both flanks. The reason was that we were the left of the whole line; beyond us on our left there was a gap of three miles through which Franco's troops could have poured if we had failed to hold the hill—a gap not filled until the next day. And it was a very considerable feat of arms for a battalion put together within a few weeks, out of men the majority of whom had no training, to hold its position without artillery or machine-gun support against a whole brigade of trained and experienced troops.

Many other days of desperate fighting followed that first day, but it stands in my memory as the symbol of our effort in Spain and our achievement.

And I think also of the cost of that achievement, and of three men, company commanders, who can be representative of those who died in the first fight on the Jarama in order that Madrid, the symbol of freedom and true democracy, should live.

These three are:

> Harry Fry of Edinburgh, at one time of His Majesty's Brigade of Guards.
>
> Kit Conway of Dublin, at one time of the Irish Republican Army.
>
> William Briskey of London, at one time of the Busman's Rank and File Movement.

They were known by the man who commanded them and by the men they commanded to be equals, in courage and comradeship, to the fighting men of the past, whose names wake pride in the British people.

Volunteer for Liberty, No. 2 February 1940, p. 4
Source: 'Marxists Internet Archive'

Appendix Four

The Nineteen Irishmen Killed at Jarama

Michael Blaser-Browne, New York

Hugh Bonar, Donegal

Danny Doyle, Belfast

Kit Conway, Tipperary

Pat Curley, Dumbarton

John Donlan, Glasgow

Charlie Donnelly, Tyrone

Bill Henry, Belfast

Robert Hilliard, Killarney

Samuel Lee, London

Thomas Morris, Boston

Paddy McDaid, Dublin

Bert McElroy, Louth

Eamonn McGrotty, Derry

Thomas O'Brien, Liverpool

Dick O'Neill, Belfast

Maurice Quinlan, Waterford

Michael Russell, Ennis

Billy Tumilson, Belfast

Appendix Five

<u>The Eleven Waterford members of the International Brigades</u>

Maurice 'Mossie' Quinlan, South Parade; Killed-in-Action, Jarama

Frank Edwards, Barrack Street

Jackie Hunt, New Street

Johnny Kelly, Grady's Lane, off Barrack Street

Harry Kennedy, Cook Lane.

Jackie Lemon, Olaf Street

Peter O'Connor, Parnell Street

John O'Shea, Johnstown

Captain Johnny Power, Newtown

Paddy Power, Newtown

Willie Power, Newtown

Appendix Six

<u>A Letter from Peter O'Connor</u>

9 Parnell St.

The Mall

Waterford

3-1-1997

Dear Liam,

Many thanks for your lovely letter which I received today. I did not seek nor do I deserve all the accolades showered on me by yourself personally and by all the Spanish people on our return to Spain for our reunion last October.

I was too embarrassed, and occasionally too ashamed to express my emotions in words.

I could not, at the time, do more than note the presence and purpose of these noble and honourable people, but nothing will erase the memory of standing side by side with them in their heroic fight against the forces of Franco and international fascism.

Even now, I feel something of the pride I felt as they thanked us, their smiles and gentle words adding to the torment of our emotions.

We were deeply affected by the very sincere friendship shown to us by all the Spanish people, especially the welcome from the young Spaniards, most of whom were not even born when the war was being waged to defeat fascism.

Thanking you again for your admiring letter, and to see you in Waterford sometime in the near future.

Comradely yours,

Peter O'Connor

Source Materials

Archives

Archive of Births, Marriages and Deaths, Werburgh Street, Dublin

Mossie Quinlan's Birth Certificate

Bureau of Military History, Defence Forces Archives

Witness Statement 1104 Thomas Brennan

Witness Statement 972 Tomás Ó Cléirigh (Thomas Cleary)

Witness Statement 783 Lieutenant-Colonel Thomas Ryan

National Archives of Ireland

Department of Foreign Affairs Files

File 141/22 Maurice Quinlan, Waterford

File 105/15 Civil War in Spain, Press Comments. March 1937

National Archives of Ireland

Calendar of Wills and Administrations 1858 - 1922

1910, p 553 Probate of Michael Reidy

UK National Archives

CO/904/100 RIC Crime Special Branch

Marx Memorial Library, London

International Brigades Association Box 21 File A

International Brigades Association Box D-7 File A/2

Rossiiskii Gosudartstvennyi Arkhiv Sotsialno-Politischeskoi Istorii RGASPI (Russian State Archive for Social and Political History).

Files are cited by fond (f.), opis (o.), delo (d.), list (l.) and scanned page.

545/2/68/139,140 545/6/66 Rapport du Camarade Leemans, Commissaire Politique, sur la Commission Irlandaise

545/2/405/26 'Map of British Battalion positions at Jarama on 12 February 1937 from Frank Ryan's 'The Book of the XV Brigade'

545/2/405/33 'Irish Fighters for Freedom', p 63 of Frank Ryan's 'The Book of the XV Brigade'

545/3/465/10 Map of British Battalion positions at Jarama on 12 February 1937

545/6/91/1 Cover of Notebook listing members of the British Battalion, 15th International Brigade alphabetically

545/6/91/30 Entry re Maurice Quinlan in Notebook listing members of the British Battalion, 15th International Brigade alphabetically

545/6/91/43 Cover of Register of members of the British Battalion, 15th International Brigade.

545/6/91/89 Entry re Maurice Quinlan in Register of members of the British Battalion, 15th International Brigade.

545/6/93/23-27 British Battalion 'Blacklist'

545/6/189/13 Personnel File references to Maurice Quinlan in two books – Frank Ryan 'The Book of the XV Brigade' p 63: *'Section Commander Leo Greene of Dublin, and Maurice Quinlan of Waterford each gave his life saving a wounded comrade.'* and William Rust 'Britons in Spain' p197

Newspapers

'Munster Express' Jan – Jun 1937

'Munster Express' 31 January 1986

'The Belfast Telegraph' 20 March 1937

'The Belfast Telegraph' Feb – Mar 1937

'The Irish Independent' Feb – Jun 1937

'The Irish Press' 20 March 1937

'The Irish Press' Feb – Jun 1937

'The Irish Times' 12 November 1917

'The Irish Times' 20 March 1937

'The Irish Times' Feb – Jun 1937

'Waterford News' 20 July 1928

'Waterford News' 1930-1937

'Waterford Standard' 27 March 1937

Bibliography

Richard Baxell, 'The British Battalion of the International Brigades in the Spanish Civil War 1936-39', Ph. D thesis, University of London, 2001

Anthony Beevor, 'The Spanish Civil War', Cassell & Co., London, 1999

Anthony Beevor, 'The Battle for Spain', Weidenfeld & Nicolson, London, 2006

William Burton, 'Faith or Antichrist – An Irishman's Diary on Irish newspapers and Franco', 'The Irish Times', 5 January 2018

Bob Doyle, 'Brigadista', Currach Press, Dublin, 2006

Aude Duche, 'You Fight Your Own Wars. Irish Defence of the Spanish Republic at War 1936-1939', Master's Thesis, Université de Haute Bretagne, Rennes, 2004

Tim Fanning, 'The Salamanca Diaries: Father McCabe and the Spanish Civil War', Irish Academic Press, Dublin, 2019

Ben Hughes, 'They Shall Not Pass! The British Battalion at Jarama', Osprey Publishing, Oxford, 2013

Walter Gregory, 'The Shallow Grave', Five Leaves Publications, Nottingham, 1996.

Michael D Higgins, *Uachtarán na hÉireann,* 'Ethical and Respectful Remembering' Speech, 12 December 2020,

https://president.ie/en/media-library/speeches

Adam Hochschild, 'Spain in Our Hearts: Americans in the Spanish Civil War 1936-1939', Houghton Mifflin Harcourt, 2016.

Raymond M Hoff, Exegesis of Robert Merriman's Diary, New York University Libraries, (online):

https://digitaltamiment.hosting.nyu.edu/files/original/5434ae298184e90c2b45d6139c10f81d072d5c41.pdf

Jim Jump, 'Poems from Spain', Lawrence & Wishart, London 2006

Anthony Keating, 'Criminal libel, censorship and contempt of court: D.C. Boyd's editorship of the Waterford Standard', In: Rafter, Kevin and O'Brien, Mark, (eds.) The State in Transition: Essays in Honour of John Horgan. New Island, Dublin, Ireland, pp. 213-234, 2015

Gustav Klaus, Ed., 'The Poetry, Life and Times of Thomas O'Brien, Volunteer in the Spanish Civil War', O'Brien Press, Dublin, 1995

Limerick International Brigades Memorial Trust, 'From the Shannon to the Ebro', 2014

Uma Arruga i López, 'Éire and España Irish Presence in the Spanish Civil War', Universitat Pompeu Fabra, Barcelona, 2020

Uinseann MacEoin, 'The IRA in the Twilight Years 1923-48', Argenta Publications, Dublin, 1997

Pat McCarthy, 'The Irish Volunteers and Waterford: part II, 1916-1919: The resistible rise of Sinn Fein', *Decies 61*, 2005

Pat McCarthy, 'The Irish Revolution 1912–23, Waterford', Four Courts Press, Dublin 2015

Pat McCarthy, 'The Redmonds and Waterford, A Political Dynasty 1891-1952', Four Courts Press, Dublin, 2018

Eamon McEneaney 'A History of Waterford and its Mayors, From the 12th Century to the 20th Century', Waterford Corporation, 1995

Barry McLoughlin, 'Colder Light on the Good Fight: Revisiting Volunteers in the Spanish Civil War', *Saothar 24*, Irish Labour History Society, 1999

Barry McLoughlin, 'Fighting for Republican Spain 1936-38', 2014.

Barry McLoughlin and Emmet O'Connor, 'In Spanish Trenches, The minds and deeds of the Irish who fought for the Republic in the Spanish Civil War', UCD Press, Dublin 2020

Manuel Montero, 'Looking for Kevin', 2014, ISBN 978-84-941750-9-1

Emmet O'Connor, 'A Labour History of Waterford', Waterford Trades Council, 1989

Emmet O'Connor, 'Mutiny or sabotage? The Irish defection to the Abraham Lincoln Battalion in the Spanish Civil War, European Social Science History Conference, 2010

Joseph O'Connor, 'Even the olives are bleeding', New Island Books, Dublin, 1992

Peter O'Connor, 'A Soldier of Liberty, Recollections of a socialist and anti-fascist fighter', MSF, Dublin 1996, Unite the UNION, Dublin, 2016

Peadar O'Donnell, 'Salud! An Irishman in Spain', Friends of the International Brigades in Ireland, 2020

Seosamh Ó Cuinneagáin, 'Saga of the Irish Brigade to Spain 1936', Donegan Print, Enniscorthy, 1975

Michael O'Riordan, 'Connolly Column', New Books, Dublin, 1979; Warren & Pell, Pontypool, 2005

George Orwell 'Homage to Catalonia', Secker and Warburg, London, 1938

Harry Owens, 'Postscript' in 'Salud! An Irishman in Spain', by Peadar O'Donnell, published by Friends of the International Brigades in Ireland, 2020

Paul Preston, 'We Saw Spain Die', Constable, London, 2008

Alejandro de Quesada, 'The Spanish Civil War 1936 – 39 (2), Republican Forces, Osprey Publishing, 2015

Seán Quinn, 'The Jarama Battle', CultureNorthernIreland.org

Frank Ryan 'Book of the XV International Brigade', Commissariat of War, XV Brigade, Madrid, 1938

David Smith, 'The man that fought the Bishop: the story of Frank Edwards and the Mount Sion Strike', *Decies 58*, 2002, pp 123 - 150

Robert A Stradling, 'The Irish and the Spanish Civil War', Manchester University Press, 1999

Hugh Thomas, 'The Spanish Civil War', Eyre & Spottiswoode, London,1962

Noel Ward, 'The Dismissal of Frank Edwards NT', '*An Múinteoir* – The Irish Teachers' Journal', Irish National Teachers' Organisation, Spring 1989

Waterford Commemoration Committee 'You are history, you are legend', 2004

Tom Wintringham, 'Comrades of Jarama', Volunteer for Liberty, No. 2 February 1940, p. 4, https://www.marxists.org/archive

Online

www.ancestry.co.uk

Caroline Angus 'This Week in the Spanish Civil War https://carolineangus.com/category/this-week-in-spanish-civil-war-history/july-1936/

Richard Baxell, 'The British Battalion at the battle of Jarama', https://richardbaxell.info/jarama/, 2010

David Convery 'There's a Valley in Spain Called Jarama'. From his Blog 'The Dustbin of History' https://thedustbinofhistory.wordpress.com/, 20 February 2013

David Crook Memoirs - Jarama www.davidcrook.net/simple/contents.html

Tramore of Yore Facebook Group

www.irishgenealogy.ie

Words of the International Brigade - The International Brigades in their own words (wordsofthebrigade.com)

Index

Previously by Liam Cahill

<u>The Centenary Edition of 'Forgotten Revolution,</u> <u>The Limerick Soviet 1919'</u>

'Forgotten Revolution' is Irish history as you have never encountered it before.

Written with the all pace and drama of a novel, it features a diverse cast of interesting and engaging people, caught up in the evolving drama of the War of Independence in 1919. Characters like Robert Byrne, the IRA hunger striker whose violent death sparks an angry response; John Cronin who leads 14,000 Limerick workers in a General Strike against the imposition of British military law; John Dowling, the radical trade union leader who turns Munster into a cauldron of red flags and soviets; the militant women workers in creameries, bakeries and mills; the Military Commandant, General Griffin, who tries to forestall the revolution; the Catholic Bishop and the Sinn Féin Mayor who manoeuvre to end the strike; national figures like Éamon de Valera, Michael Collins and Richard Mulcahy.

For two weeks, the workers' committee – The Soviet – rule Limerick. They control foodstuffs, prices, transport, print their own newspaper and even their own currency. For a time, in April 1919, they pose a major threat to British power in Ireland.

'Forgotten Revolution' is a great achievement and an important book'.

– Professor Diarmaid Ferriter, UCD

• **Signed copies on sale now from** <u>www.buythebook.ie</u>
• **€15 +Postage**